STRESS MANAGEMENT TOOLS

COPING WITH STRESS FOR MENTAL AND
PHYSICAL HEALTH AND LONGEVITY

FUNCTIONAL HEALTH SERIES

SAM FURY

Copyright SF Nonfiction Books © 2023

www.SFNonfictionBooks.com

All Rights Reserved
No part of this document may be reproduced without written consent from the author.

WARNINGS AND DISCLAIMERS

The information in this publication is made public for reference only.

Neither the author, publisher, nor anyone else involved in the production of this publication is responsible for how the reader uses the information or the result of his/her actions.

Nothing presented is medical advice. Implement anything you learn at your own risk. If in doubt, please consult a medical professional.

CONTENTS

Introduction	vii
Types of Stress	1
Stress Hormones	4
Identifying Stress Triggers	5
Genetics and Personality in Stress	15
Cultural Aspects of Stress	17
Stress and Physical Health	19
Chronic Stress and Mental Health	21
Impact of Technology on Stress	25
Unhealthy Coping Mechanisms	29
Creating a Relaxing Environment	35
Creating a Supportive Environment	42
Physical Activity and Stress	48
Diet and Nutrition	51
Time Management Skills	54
Breathing Exercises	64
Progressive Muscle Relaxation	68
Mindfulness and Meditation	71
Cognitive Behavioral Techniques	78
Biofeedback and Stress	80
Alternative Therapies	83
Hormesis	88
Stress Management Techniques For Children	93
Creating Your Stress Management Plan	96
Conclusion	100
About Sam Fury	103
References	104

All books in the Functional Health Series are transcriptions of masterclasses from within our members area.

As a member, you will get full access to all these masterclasses in eBook and audio format and a whole lot more at no extra cost.

Get 30 days access for just $1!

www.functionalhealth.coach/members

INTRODUCTION

Stress, by definition, is the body's response to any demand or challenge. While occasional stress can be beneficial, providing a burst of energy or heightened alertness, chronic stress can have profound effects on both mind and body. It can disrupt nearly every system in your body, leading to health problems like heart disease, sleep disturbances, digestive issues, obesity, and a weakened immune system. The mind is equally affected, with chronic stress contributing to anxiety, depression, and other mental health disorders.

Understanding stress requires a multifaceted approach. We are going to explore different types of stress and the role of stress hormones like cortisol and adrenaline, which are crucial for short-term responses but detrimental when elevated over long periods. We'll delve into the process of identifying stress triggers, considering how genetics, personality, and cultural aspects influence our response to stress. It's important to recognize how stress impacts physical health, contributing to conditions like hypertension and diabetes, and mental health, where it can exacerbate or trigger psychological issues.

However, stress is not an invincible foe. Effective stress management can lead to numerous benefits, including improved physical health, mental well-being, and overall quality of life. You will be provided with a comprehensive overview of various stress management techniques. We'll cover the creation of relaxing and supportive environments, both at home and in the workplace, emphasizing the importance of physical activity, diet, and nutrition in stress reduction. Time management skills, breathing exercises, and progressive muscle relaxation are practical tools that can be incorporated into daily routines. Additionally, we'll delve into mindfulness, meditation, cognitive behavioral techniques, and even biofeedback, exploring how these methods can help in recognizing and altering stress responses.

Alternative therapies and the concept of hormesis, where moderate stressors can actually strengthen the body's stress response, will also be discussed. Special attention is given to stress management in children, emphasizing the need for early intervention. And then everything culminates in guiding you to create a personalized stress management plan, fostering long-term resilience and recovery.

In essence, you will embark on a thorough exploration of stress and its management, from identifying triggers to implementing practical strategies in various aspects of life. By the end, you'll not only understand stress better but also be equipped with a diverse range of techniques to manage it effectively, leading to a healthier, more balanced life.

TYPES OF STRESS

Imagine you're faced with a big presentation at work, and you haven't prepared as well as you'd like. You're feeling jittery, your heart's racing, and you're sweating a bit - that's acute stress kicking in. It's your body's natural response to a perceived threat or challenge. Acute stress is usually short-term, and it can actually be beneficial in small doses. It can help you stay alert and focused in the moment.

Now, let's shift gears to chronic stress. Picture this: you've been dealing with a demanding job, financial troubles, and relationship issues for months on end. It's like a never-ending cycle of stress that just won't let up. This is chronic stress, and it's a whole different ballgame. Unlike acute stress, chronic stress sticks around for the long haul, and it can take a serious toll on your physical and mental health.

Studies have shown that acute stress, when managed properly, can actually be motivating. It can push you to perform better under pressure. But if it becomes chronic, it's like a slow burn that can lead to serious health problems. Chronic stress has been linked to heart disease, high blood pressure, depression, and even a weakened immune system. It's like your body is stuck in "fight or flight" mode for an extended period, which isn't good.

To put it in perspective, think about a story. Let's say you have a friend named Sarah. She's a student who's always had a knack for handling the stress of exams. When the final exams roll around, Sarah feels that acute stress kick in. It helps her focus, study harder, and do her best. Once the exams are over, that acute stress subsides, and she can relax.

Now, let's look at another friend, John. He's in a job that demands long hours, tight deadlines, and constant pressure. Day in and day out, John faces chronic stress. Over time, it starts affecting his sleep, his mood, and his overall health. Unlike Sarah's short-lived stress during exams, John's stress is ongoing, and that's what makes it chronic.

In short, acute stress is a short-term response to a specific challenge, and it can be a bit of a motivator. Chronic stress, on the other hand, is a long-lasting burden that can lead to serious health issues if not managed. Remember, it's important to find healthy ways to cope with stress, whether it's acute or chronic, because taking care of your well-being is always a priority.

Now let's dive into emotional, physical, and environmental stressors. Think of them as the different types of challenges life can throw at you, each with its own way of affecting your well-being.

First up, emotional stressors. These are like the feelings and thoughts that can really get under your skin. Imagine you're going through a tough breakup or dealing with the loss of a loved one. Those emotions can create emotional stress. Studies have shown that ongoing emotional stress can lead to things like anxiety and depression. So, it's crucial to find healthy ways to cope with these feelings, like talking to friends or seeking professional help.

Now, let's talk physical stressors. These are all about your body. Think of when you're not getting enough sleep or you're pushing yourself too hard at the gym. Your body takes a toll, right? That's physical stress. It can weaken your immune system, disrupt your sleep patterns, and even cause chronic pain. It's like your body's way of saying, "Hey, slow down and take care of me!" So, it's important to listen to your body and give it the rest and care it needs.

Lastly, there are environmental stressors. These are external factors that can mess with your peace of mind. Picture a noisy construction site outside your window or a cramped and cluttered workspace. These situations can create environmental stress. Research has shown that exposure to chronic noise or a chaotic environment can increase stress hormones in your body. To deal with this type of stressor, you might need to create a more soothing and organized environment or use earplugs to drown out the noise.

Imagine you have a friend named Alex. He's going through a challenging time at work, which is an emotional stressor, and he's also juggling a busy schedule that leaves them tired and sore, which is a physical stressor. On top of that, he lives in a noisy apartment building, which is an environmental stressor). All these stressors are piling up, and Alex starts feeling overwhelmed.

Luckily, Alex realizes the potential damage that could be done and takes action. He starts talking to a therapist to manage the emotional stress, prioritizes self-care to address the physical stress, and even considers noise-canceling headphones to tackle the environmental stress. Over time, he starts feeling more balanced and less stressed.

Life can throw all different types of stressors at you, but there are ways to cope and find balance. It's all about recognizing what's stressing you out and taking steps to address it in a healthy way.

STRESS HORMONES

Our bodies have a natural response to stress, and hormones play a big role in that.

One of the key stress hormones is cortisol. When we're stressed, our body releases cortisol, which helps us deal with the immediate stressor. It increases our energy levels and helps with our fight-or-flight response. But if we're constantly stressed, high levels of cortisol can have negative effects on our health. Research has shown that chronic stress and elevated cortisol levels can lead to problems like high blood pressure, weight gain, and even memory issues.

Another important stress hormone is adrenaline, also known as epinephrine. This one gets our heart racing and makes us more alert when we're faced with a stressful situation. It's like our body's way of getting us ready to react quickly. But just like with cortisol, too much adrenaline for too long can put a strain on our heart and have negative health effects.

There's also norepinephrine, which works alongside adrenaline. It helps to narrow our blood vessels, raising our blood pressure. This can be helpful in short bursts when we need to respond to a stressor, but prolonged high levels of norepinephrine can be harmful and contribute to conditions like hypertension.

And lastly, oxytocin. It's often called the "love hormone" because it's released when we bond with others, like during a hug or when we're feeling close to someone. Interestingly, it can also be released in response to stress. Research has shown that oxytocin can have a calming effect during stressful times, promoting social bonding and support.

Stress hormones like cortisol, adrenaline, and norepinephrine help our bodies respond to stress by increasing alertness and energy. But chronic stress can lead to an overproduction of these hormones, which can have negative effects on our health. On the flip side, oxytocin can have a calming influence during stressful moments.

IDENTIFYING STRESS TRIGGERS

Identifying your personal stress triggers is super important for your well-being. It's like having a map to navigate through life's challenges. Let me tell you why it's so crucial.

Firstly, when you know what stresses you out, you can take steps to avoid or manage those situations better. A study in the "Journal of Behavioral Medicine" found that people who identified their stressors had lower stress levels overall. It's like knowing there's a traffic jam on your route and finding an alternative way to reach your destination faster.

Secondly, recognizing your stress triggers helps you take control of your emotional and physical health. Stress can mess with your body in many ways, from headaches to heart problems. Understanding what sets off your stress can empower you to make healthier choices.

Thirdly, it improves your relationships. When you know what stresses you, you can communicate your needs better to your loved ones. They can also understand you more, which can lead to less conflict. In fact, a study in the "Journal of Marriage and Family" in 2015 found that couples who identified stressors together had more satisfaction in their relationships.

Lastly, identifying stress triggers can boost your overall happiness. It lets you focus on what truly matters and invest your time and energy wisely. Knowing your triggers helps you work on personal growth and resilience.

Pinpointing your stress triggers is like having a superpower for your well-being. It helps you avoid stress, manage it better, improve your health, nurture relationships, and ultimately be a happier you.

Stress can come from all sorts of places, and it's different for everyone. Work can be a big source of stress for many of us, and it's vital to understand what gets those stress gears turning.

One study in the "Journal of Occupational Health Psychology" dives into this topic. They found that work-related stress can seriously mess with your well-being and performance. So, what are these stress triggers at work? Well, here are some common ones:

First up, there's the pressure of deadlines. When you're racing against the clock to finish tasks, it can really amp up your stress levels. Multiple tight deadlines can make you feel like you're in a pressure cooker.

Then there are those demanding bosses. If your boss is always breathing down your neck, criticizing your every move, or setting impossible expectations, that's a major stressor. It can make you feel constantly on edge.

Heavy workloads can also pile on the stress. When you've got more tasks than you can handle, it's like trying to juggle too many balls at once. It can leave you feeling overwhelmed and exhausted.

Workplace conflicts and office politics are no picnic either. Dealing with colleagues or superiors who don't get along with you can be really stressful. Plus, navigating office politics and power struggles can be a headache.

Job insecurity is another big one. If you're worried about losing your job or don't have job stability, it can be super stressful. You might fret about your finances and what the future holds.

Feeling like you have no control over your work or your work environment? That's a stress trigger too. It's tough when decisions are made without your input, or you're given tasks that aren't in your wheelhouse.

And don't forget those long commutes! Spending hours stuck in traffic or on crowded buses can be draining. It's like starting and ending your workday with an extra dose of stress.

Now, let's talk about the impact of all this stress. When work-related stress gets the better of you, it can lead to health problems like high blood pressure and digestive issues. It's not just physical – your mental health can take a hit too, with anxiety and depression becoming real risks.

Work performance can also suffer. Stress can mess with your ability to focus, make decisions, and perform well. That could affect your job and your chances of moving up the career ladder.

If things get really tough, you might even face burnout – a state of emotional exhaustion, reduced motivation, and feeling disconnected from your work. It's a sign that stress has taken over.

And remember, work stress doesn't stay confined to the office. It can seep into your personal life, causing trouble in your relationships and overall quality of life.

Financial stress is another common source of stress, and it's no surprise. When you're grappling with money problems, it can make your stress levels soar. It's essential to understand what's going on in your financial world and how it's impacting your well-being.

One thing to keep in mind is that financial stress isn't just about not having enough money. It can come from various sources.

First off, there's the struggle to make ends meet. When your income isn't covering your basic expenses like rent, bills, and groceries, it's a recipe for anxiety. It's like a constant worry hanging over your head.

Debt is another major player in financial stress. Whether it's credit card debt, student loans, or medical bills, owing money can be incredibly stressful. The pressure to pay it all off can feel overwhelming.

And let's not forget about unexpected expenses. When surprise costs pop up, like car repairs or medical emergencies, it can throw your financial stability into chaos. It's like a curveball that you didn't see coming.

So, what can you do about financial stress? Well, the first step is acknowledging it. Once you recognize that money worries are stressing you out, you can start taking action. This might include creating a budget, seeking financial advice, or exploring debt management strategies.

Remember, you're not alone in facing financial stress. Many people go through it at some point. The key is to reach out for help and find solutions that work for you. Your well-being matters, and managing financial stress is a big part of taking care of yourself.

Next up, relationships. Relationships are a big part of our lives, and when they hit rough patches, it can bring a lot of stress into the picture. Whether it's conflicts with family members, partners, or friends, these issues can take a toll on your emotional well-being.

Let's start with conflicts. When you have disagreements, arguments, or misunderstandings with the people you care about, it can be emotionally draining. It's like a weight on your shoulders, and it can make you feel upset, frustrated, or even angry.

Family conflicts can be particularly challenging. These are the people you're often closest to, so when there's tension or disagreement within the family, it can hit you hard. It might be disagreements over values, lifestyle choices, or other issues.

Relationship problems with your partner can be incredibly stressful too. Whether it's communication breakdowns, trust issues, or differences in goals, these challenges can strain your emotional well-being. It can feel like you're walking on eggshells or constantly in turmoil.

Even problems with friends can bring their share of stress. Friendships are essential for social support and connection, so when these relationships sour, it can lead to feelings of loneliness and isolation.

As with most forms of stress, the first step is recognizing it and acknowledging the problems. Communication is often key. Try to have open and honest conversations with the people involved, and consider seeking help from a therapist or counselor if needed.

Remember that it's okay to reach out for support, whether from friends, family, or professionals. Building healthy communication skills and working towards resolving conflicts can improve your emotional well-being and the quality of your relationships.

Health problems, whether they affect you personally or a loved one, can be incredibly stressful. It's natural to worry when it comes to matters of health, and the fear and uncertainty that often accompany illness can be very challenging to cope with.

When it's your own health at stake, a diagnosis or even just the suspicion of a health issue can be a significant stress trigger. It can bring up questions like, "What's going to happen to me?" or "How will this impact my life?" These uncertainties can create anxiety and emotional turmoil.

When a loved one is facing health issues, it can be just as stressful. You might feel helpless or overwhelmed, not knowing how to provide the support they need. Witnessing someone you care about go through pain or suffering can be emotionally draining.

If it's your own health, consult with a healthcare provider who can provide accurate information, guidance, and a treatment plan. If it's a loved one, support and care from healthcare professionals can be invaluable.

In addition to seeking medical advice, consider seeking emotional support. Talking to a therapist or counselor can help you manage the emotional toll of health issues and develop coping strategies.

Remember that it's okay to reach out to friends and family for support as well. They can be a source of comfort and assistance during challenging times.

Daily hassles, those small but irritating things like traffic jams, long queues, or just the little annoyances that seem to pop up every day, can really add to your stress load too. It's these minor inconveniences that we often brush off individually, but when they pile up, they can become a significant source of stress.

One study published in the "Journal of Applied Psychology" even suggests that these daily hassles can make a big contribution to your overall stress levels. So, let's take a closer look at how they can affect you.

First off, traffic jams are a classic example. Sitting in bumper-to-bumper traffic, especially during rush hour, can be incredibly frustrating. It's like a daily test of your patience. And if you're running late for work or an important appointment, it can crank up the stress meter.

Long queues, whether at the grocery store, the bank, or any other place, can also be a hassle. Waiting in line when you're in a hurry or have other things to do can be aggravating. It's one of those situations where you just wish you could fast forward time.

Then there are the small annoyances, like your computer freezing or spilling your coffee in the morning. While they may seem trivial, they can contribute to your overall stress, especially when they happen repeatedly.

Over time, these small stressors can accumulate and contribute to your overall stress levels. It's like having a backpack filled with rocks – each hassle adds weight, and eventually, it can feel overwhelming.

One approach to combat these small stressors is to practice stress management techniques like deep breathing or mindfulness to help you stay calm in the moment.

It's also helpful to keep things in perspective. Try not to sweat the small stuff, and remind yourself that these daily hassles are just temporary inconveniences.

Additionally, planning ahead and leaving a bit earlier for appointments can help you avoid the stress of running late due to traffic or long queues.

Lastly, major life changes such as moving, getting married, or having a baby can also be stress triggers. These events can bring a mix of excitement and anxiety.

Let's break down these life changes and how they can impact your stress levels.

First, moving to a new location. Whether it's for a job, a fresh start, or any other reason, relocating can be stressful. It involves leaving behind familiar surroundings, friends, and routines. The process of packing, unpacking, and adjusting to a new environment can be overwhelming.

Getting married is another major life change. While it's a joyful event, planning a wedding can be incredibly stressful. There are many details to manage, family expectations to navigate, and financial considerations to address. The transition from single life to married life also brings its own set of adjustments and challenges.

Having a baby is a life-altering experience. The anticipation of a new addition to the family is exciting, but it can also be accompanied by anxiety. Pregnancy, childbirth, and the responsibilities of parenthood can create physical, emotional, and financial stress. Sleepless nights and the demands of caring for a newborn can add to the pressure.

There are several things you can do to manage the stress associated with major life changes.

When possible, plan ahead for these changes. Create a budget, make a to-do list, and seek support from friends and family.

Also, make sure you share your feelings and concerns with loved ones or consider talking to a therapist. Emotional support can make a significant difference during times of change.

And don't forget to take care of yourself. Prioritize self-care and stress management techniques like exercise, mindfulness, and relaxation.

Finally, stay flexible. Be open to adjusting your plans and expectations as needed. Change can be unpredictable, so adaptability is a valuable skill.

Now that you know what some common stress triggers are, and have a general idea of what you can do to combat them, let's give you some tools you can use to identify your personal stress triggers.

The first is self-reflection. Taking some quiet time to reflect on recent stressful experiences can be a valuable tool. This introspective approach allows you to gain insights into what specifically causes you stress, helping you develop strategies to cope better.

One effective method for self-reflection is journaling. When you write down your thoughts and feelings during stressful situations, you create a record of your experiences. This written record helps you recognize patterns in your stress triggers over time. It allows you to pinpoint common themes or situations that consistently lead to stress.

During your quiet reflection time, consider various aspects of recent stressful events. Think about the situations, people, or events that made you feel uneasy or anxious. Try to recall the physical and emotional sensations you experienced. Were there any specific thoughts or worries that stood out? By delving deep into these details, you can uncover the root causes of your stress.

As you continue this process, you may start to notice common themes emerging from your reflections. For example, you might find that interactions with a particular person consistently lead to stress, or that work-related deadlines trigger anxiety.

Stress surveys and assessments are also valuable tools for identifying and understanding your stress triggers. They provide a structured way to evaluate various aspects of your life that might be contributing to stress. Many online stress assessments are readily accessible and can help pinpoint specific stressors.

These assessments typically consist of a series of questions designed to gauge your stress levels and identify potential stressors. Questions often cover areas such as work, relationships, finances, and physical health. By responding to these questions honestly, you can gain insights into the sources of your stress.

Tracking physical symptoms is another effective approach for identifying stress triggers on your own. Stress often manifests itself through physical symptoms like headaches, muscle tension, stomach issues, and more. By paying close attention to your body's reactions during stressful times, you can gain valuable insights into the sources of your stress.

When you experience stress, your body responds with various physiological reactions. These can include increased heart rate, shallow breathing, or even sweating. By noticing these physical cues, you can start to connect them to specific situations or events that trigger your stress.

Research in psychophysiology has shown that our bodies react to stress in consistent ways. For instance, a study published in the journal Psychosomatic Medicine found that stress can lead to changes in heart rate variability, which is a measurable physiological response. This highlights the strong connection between stress and physical symptoms.

Seeking support from loved ones is a helpful strategy when you need assistance in identifying your stress triggers. Talking to trusted friends or family members about your experiences can provide fresh perspectives and insights into what might be causing your stress. Those close to you may observe patterns or triggers that you haven't noticed on your own.

When you engage in conversations with loved ones about your stressors, it allows you to see your experiences from different angles. They may offer observations or feedback that help you connect the dots between specific situations and your stress reactions. This collaborative effort can be particularly valuable in uncovering hidden stress triggers.

Additionally, discussing your stress with loved ones can strengthen your emotional bonds and create a supportive network. It fosters a sense of connection and understanding, which can be comforting during stressful times.

Consulting a therapist or counselor is a highly beneficial option for pinpointing and managing stress triggers. These professionals offer a safe and confidential environment where you can delve into your emotions and gain insights into what might be causing your stress.

Therapists and counselors are trained to help individuals navigate their emotions and identify underlying stressors. They use various therapeutic techniques and approaches to assist you in understanding the root causes of your stress. Studies and research consistently emphasize the effectiveness of therapy in managing stress and improving mental well-being.

In therapy, you have the opportunity to discuss your experiences, thoughts, and feelings openly. Therapists can guide you in exploring your stress triggers, helping you recognize patterns, and offering strategies to cope with them effectively. They can also provide valuable coping mechanisms and tools tailored to your specific needs.

The therapeutic process often involves self-reflection, self-discovery, and personal growth. Over time, you can gain a deeper understanding of yourself and the factors that contribute to your stress. This knowledge empowers you to make informed choices and develop healthier ways to manage stress.

Remember, identifying your stress triggers is a journey, and it might require a combination of these tools. It's all about finding what works best for you.

GENETICS AND PERSONALITY IN STRESS

Stress is an inevitable part of life, and how we react to it can vary widely from person to person. Two crucial factors that play a significant role in how we respond to stress are genetics and personality. Our genes can influence how our bodies and brains react to stressors, while our personality traits can determine our coping mechanisms.

Imagine you and your friend face a stressful situation, like a challenging exam or a tight work deadline. You might notice that your friend seems to get more anxious or down in the dumps than you do. Well, genetics could be playing a part in that difference.

Research, like a study published in the "Psychological Bulletin" in 2013, has shown that certain gene variations related to the serotonin system can affect how people respond to stress. Serotonin is a brain chemical that helps regulate mood. People with specific gene variations may have lower serotonin levels, making them more vulnerable to anxiety and depression when faced with stressful situations. So, when your friend gets stressed out, it might be because of these genetic factors that make them more sensitive to stress.

But it's not just about how we feel emotionally. Genetics can also influence how our bodies physically react to stress. You might have heard of the "fight-or-flight" response, which is like our body's alarm system when we encounter a stressful situation. This response is controlled by our autonomic nervous system. Here's where genetics come into play again.

In 2019, a study published in "Psychoneuroendocrinology" found specific gene variants that can crank up the volume on our stress responses. When these gene variants are in the mix, our bodies may produce more cortisol, which is a hormone linked to stress. So, when some individuals experience stress, their genetic makeup can lead to higher cortisol levels and a prolonged stress reaction.

Our personalities also play a significant role in how we handle stress. In fact, researchers have pinpointed specific personality traits that can affect how we cope with stress.

One important personality trait is neuroticism. Individuals with high levels of neuroticism tend to be more prone to stress. They may worry a lot, feel anxious, or get upset easily when faced with stressful situations. It can be tougher for them to manage stress effectively.

On the flip side, some personality traits can be like natural stress-fighting superheroes. Extraversion and conscientiousness are two such traits. People with high extraversion are outgoing and sociable, which can help them build strong support networks. This can be super helpful in times of stress. Conscientious folks are organized and reliable, so they tend to plan ahead and handle stress with a positive attitude.

In 2017, the "Journal of Personality and Social Psychology" published research on how different personality traits influence the way we cope with stress. It discovered that individuals with higher levels of openness to experience often use problem-solving and emotion-focused coping strategies. They're the kind of people who think creatively to find solutions or express their feelings when dealing with stress.

On the other hand, those with higher levels of neuroticism sometimes turn to avoidant coping mechanisms when stress hits. This might involve denial, trying to ignore the problem, or even using substances like alcohol or drugs to escape from stress temporarily. It's like their way of putting up a shield against stress, but it's not always the most effective approach.

Both genetic factors and personality types can significantly impact our responses to stress. Genetics can influence our predisposition to stress-related disorders and our physiological reactions, while personality traits can shape our coping mechanisms and overall resilience. Understanding these factors can help individuals develop more effective strategies for managing stress in their lives.

CULTURAL ASPECTS OF STRESS

Stress is a universal human experience, but the way it's perceived and managed can vary significantly across different cultures. Understanding these cultural aspects of stress is essential in today's diverse world, as it helps us empathize with others and adapt our approaches to stress management. Let's delve into how various cultures perceive and cope with stress.

In some Western cultures, such as the United States and many European countries, stress is often seen as a consequence of a fast-paced, competitive lifestyle. People in these cultures may prioritize individualism and self-reliance when dealing with stress. They might turn to professional therapy, support groups, or self-help books to manage their stress. Moreover, exercise and mindfulness techniques like meditation have gained popularity as stress-reduction strategies in these regions.

In contrast, collectivist cultures, like those found in many Asian countries, often emphasize harmony within the community. Stress is often seen as a shared burden. Individuals in such cultures may be more inclined to rely on social support from family and friends. Practices like yoga, tai chi, or traditional meditation techniques are frequently used to manage stress. Additionally, cultural rituals and religious practices play a significant role in providing a sense of purpose and calm during difficult times.

African and indigenous cultures have unique approaches to stress as well. These cultures often emphasize the importance of connection with nature and spirituality. Healing ceremonies, storytelling, and communal gatherings are common ways to cope with stress. Traditional healers and elders often play essential roles in guiding individuals through stressful situations, focusing on holistic well-being.

In some Middle Eastern cultures, where religion plays a central role, faith and prayer are vital components of stress management. Believers often find solace and resilience in their religious practices.

Additionally, the extended family network is crucial in providing emotional support and practical assistance during challenging times.

It's essential to recognize that within each culture, there can be variations in how individuals perceive and manage stress based on factors like age, gender, socioeconomic status, and personal beliefs. Moreover, globalization and increased cultural exchange are influencing how people approach stress worldwide, leading to a blending of strategies and beliefs.

Cultural aspects of stress are diverse and fascinating, reflecting the rich tapestry of human experience. By acknowledging and respecting these cultural differences, we can better support one another in times of stress and promote mental well-being on a global scale.

STRESS AND PHYSICAL HEALTH

Stress is a common part of life, but when it becomes chronic, it can take a toll on our physical health. While a little stress can actually be motivating, long-term stress can lead to various health problems.

First of all, chronic stress can significantly impact the immune system. When you're stressed for a long time, your body starts releasing stress hormones, like cortisol. Now, cortisol isn't all bad; it helps you deal with short-term stress, but when it hangs around too long, it can weaken your immune response.

In a study published in the "Psychological Bulletin" by Segerstrom and Miller back in 2004, they found some interesting stuff. They discovered that chronic stress can actually suppress your immune system's ability to fight off infections. So, when you're constantly stressed, your body might not be as good at defending itself against those pesky germs.

Your heart health can also suffer under the weight of chronic stress. When you're stressed, your body releases hormones that can narrow your blood vessels and make your heart pump harder. Over time, this can strain your heart and raise your risk of heart disease.

There's some research published in the journal "Circulation" by Rosengren and colleagues back in 2004 that looked into this. They found that people with high levels of stress were more likely to develop heart problems as time went on. It's a bit like your heart is working overtime when you're stressed, and if it keeps doing that for too long, it can lead to some serious issues.

Now let's talk about how chronic stress can make chronic pain even tougher to deal with. If you're already dealing with conditions like arthritis or chronic back pain, stress can be like adding fuel to the fire. This is because when you're stressed over a long period, it can mess with how you perceive pain. There's a study published in the "Journal of Psychosomatic Research" by McAllister and colleagues in 2007 that looked into this. They found that stress can make you feel pain more intensely. It's like your body becomes more sensitive to pain signals, so those aches and pains you already have can feel even worse.

But that's not all; stress can also make it harder to manage chronic pain. When you're stressed out, you might find it challenging to relax and find relief. It's a bit like a vicious cycle - pain causes stress, and stress makes the pain worse.

Lastly, stress can affect your stomach and gut too.

When you're under chronic stress, it can lead to some pretty uncomfortable gastrointestinal problems, such as irritable bowel syndrome, otherwise known as **IBS**. You know that feeling when your stomach is all upset, and you're dealing with things like abdominal pain, diarrhea, or constipation? Well, chronic stress can make those symptoms worse and even trigger them in some cases.

There's a study published in the journal "Gut" by Koloski and colleagues in 2008 that dug into this connection. They found a strong link between chronic stress and the development of **IBS** symptoms. It's like your digestive system gets all worked up when you're stressed out, and it doesn't function as smoothly as it should.

CHRONIC STRESS AND MENTAL HEALTH

Chronic stress and mental health are closely intertwined, and understanding this relationship is crucial for maintaining overall well-being. Stress is a natural response to challenging situations, but when it becomes chronic – persisting over an extended period – it can have detrimental effects on mental health. Numerous studies have shown that chronic stress can contribute to the development and exacerbation of mental health disorders like depression, anxiety, and more.

When we talk about chronic stress, we're talking about those never-ending sources of stress that can creep into our lives. It could be related to our jobs, the ups and downs in our relationships, financial worries that keep us up at night, or even health problems that persist. Chronic stress isn't the kind of stress that comes and goes – it's the stress that sticks around like an unwelcome guest.

Now, when it comes to mental health, one of the most prominent conditions linked to chronic stress is depression. Research has been pretty consistent in showing that there's a connection between chronic stress and an increased risk of developing depression. A study published in the journal "Psychological Medicine" back in 2017 took a closer look at this. What they found was that people exposed to chronic stressors were more likely to experience depressive symptoms. It's like chronic stress can gradually chip away at our mental well-being and contribute to the onset of depression.

When you're constantly dealing with stress – be it from a demanding job, troubled relationships, financial strains, or health issues – it's like carrying a heavy load on your shoulders day in and day out. Over time, that load can become overwhelming, and it can start to affect your mood, your thoughts, and how you feel about yourself. That's why we often see depression and chronic stress going hand in hand.

When we talk about anxiety disorders, we're referring to conditions where people often feel excessive worry, fear, or nervousness. Now, chronic stress plays a significant role in these anxiety disorders. When someone faces long-term stress, it can rev up their stress response system – that's the part of our body that kicks into action when we feel threatened. But here's the thing: chronic stress can make this system overactive, like an alarm that's always going off.

This overactive stress response can cause individuals to feel anxious and overwhelmed, even when there's no immediate danger around. It's like their body and mind are on high alert all the time. Imagine always being on edge, worrying about what might happen next, or even having panic attacks seemingly out of nowhere – that's how chronic stress can impact anxiety disorders.

What makes this particularly challenging is that chronic stress can create a vicious cycle with anxiety. When you're constantly stressed, it can trigger anxiety symptoms, and in turn, anxiety can make you more sensitive to stress. It's like a never-ending loop that can be tough to break free from.

Chronic stress can also really mess with your sleep. Studies have shown that people who deal with ongoing stress are more likely to develop insomnia. It's like a vicious cycle – stress keeps you awake at night, and then not getting enough sleep can make you even more stressed during the day.

One reason for this is that stress can mess with your body's production of hormones, like cortisol. High cortisol levels due to chronic stress can make it harder for you to relax and fall asleep when bedtime rolls around. Plus, stress can get your mind racing with worries and thoughts, making it tough to wind down.

Another thing is that when you're stressed, your body's fight-or-flight response is activated, and that's not the ideal state for bedtime. Your heart rate goes up, and your body stays alert, which is the opposite of what you need to drift off peacefully.

The worse thing is that when you don't get enough sleep because of chronic stress, it can make your stress levels even worse the next day.

You're more irritable, less able to cope with stressors, and it's a recipe for more sleepless nights.

Studies have also shown that chronic stress can increase the risk of developing substance abuse issues. When you're stressed for a long time, your brain chemistry can change. Stress messes with the reward centers in your brain, making you more likely to seek out things that make you feel good, like drugs or alcohol.

Plus, chronic stress can weaken your self-control and decision-making abilities. So, when you're faced with a choice about using substances, you might be more likely to give in to the temptation because your ability to say no is compromised.

Another thing to consider is that people often turn to substances to numb the emotional pain caused by chronic stress. They might use drugs or alcohol as a way to escape their worries temporarily. This can lead to a dangerous cycle, where the substance use provides short-term relief, but in the long run, it worsens both the stress and the substance abuse.

It's important to note that not everyone who experiences chronic stress will develop a substance abuse disorder, but the risk is higher. So, managing stress is crucial in preventing these issues.

Chronic stress can also contribute to cognitive decline, especially in older adults. When you're under prolonged stress, your body produces high levels of stress hormones like cortisol. These hormones can affect your brain in ways that aren't so great for your cognitive function.

One way this happens is through the shrinking of the hippocampus, a part of your brain that's crucial for memory. Chronic stress can actually lead to the hippocampus getting smaller over time, which is not what we want for good memory and thinking skills.

Moreover, stress can mess with the connections between brain cells, making it harder for them to communicate effectively. This can lead to problems with concentration, learning, and memory retention.

Chronic stress can also contribute to unhealthy habits like poor sleep, overeating, and not exercising – all of which can further increase the risk of cognitive decline. So, it's like a double whammy.

Finally, let's explore how chronic stress can worsen existing mental health conditions, like post-traumatic stress disorder (PTSD). It's an important aspect to understand.

Someone with PTSD has often experienced a traumatic event that left a deep impact on their mental well-being. They might already have symptoms like flashbacks, nightmares, or severe anxiety. Now, when chronic stress enters the picture, it's like pouring fuel on the fire. The ongoing stressors can intensify their existing symptoms, making it even more challenging for them to cope.

There was a study published in the "Journal of Traumatic Stress" in 2013 that looked into this very issue. They discussed how chronic stress can have a profound impact on individuals with PTSD, making their symptoms more severe. This research also highlighted the importance of stress management in the treatment of PTSD.

So, the bottom line here is that chronic stress isn't just a standalone issue; it can make existing mental health conditions, like PTSD, much more difficult to manage. Recognizing this connection underscores the importance of addressing both chronic stress and the underlying mental health condition for effective treatment.

The relationship between chronic stress and mental health is well-established through various research studies. Chronic stress can contribute to the development of mental health disorders such as depression, anxiety, and can exacerbate existing conditions like PTSD. Recognizing the connection between chronic stress and mental health is one of the first steps towards finding effective strategies to manage stress and promote mental well-being.

IMPACT OF TECHNOLOGY ON STRESS

There's no doubt that technology has become an integral part of our daily lives. From smartphones to social media platforms and the digital realm, these innovations have undoubtedly brought convenience and connectivity. However, they have also introduced a new set of challenges, particularly when it comes to our stress levels.

You wake up in the morning, and as soon as you open your eyes, your smartphone is buzzing with emails, text messages, and social media notifications. Throughout the day, you're bombarded with a constant stream of digital information. It's like a never-ending waterfall of data pouring into your brain.

This overload of information can really mess with our heads. A study published in the journal "Computers in Human Behavior" found that when we're exposed to too much information, it can crank up our stress levels and even lower our overall sense of well-being. It's like our brains are trying to juggle too many balls at once, and it's exhausting.

When you're trying to read an important email or concentrate on a task, those constant pings and notifications can break your focus. It's like someone keeps tapping you on the shoulder while you're trying to work or relax. And this interruption can lead to frustration and stress.

Plus, there's this sense of urgency that comes with technology. We feel like we need to respond to every message or check every update immediately. It's like there's an invisible pressure pushing us to stay connected 24/7. That feeling of being 'always on' can leave us feeling drained and stressed.

Now let's look into how social media, while keeping us connected and informed, can also be a source of stress. A study published in the "Journal of Abnormal Psychology" found that young adults who spend excessive amounts of time on social media tend to experience higher levels of depression and anxiety. One big reason for this is the constant comparison game. When we see our friends' highlight reels, it's easy to feel like we're falling short in comparison. It's like we're in a never-ending competition, and that can really take a toll on our self-esteem and happiness.

Then, there's the fear of missing out, often called FOMO. It's that feeling you get when you see your friends having fun without you. FOMO can make us anxious and even make us question our social worth. It's crazy how a few posts and photos can stir up so much stress!

And let's not forget about cyberbullying. Social media isn't always a friendly place, and the negativity, hate comments, and online harassment can be incredibly distressing. It's like dealing with bullies, but now they can reach you wherever you are.

Another major shift is the increase in remote work and online learning. While these developments offer convenience, they've also blurred the lines between our work or school life and our personal life. This blending can lead to chronic stress, where it becomes really tough to disconnect from our tasks and just relax. It's not just something we feel; studies have found evidence of this in people's lives.

Furthermore, our constant connection to digital devices has given rise to what's often called an "always-on" culture. This means we're reachable and working or studying around the clock, thanks to our smartphones and computers. But this constant connectivity can mess with our sleep patterns. A study published in the "Journal of Sleep Research" showed that disruptions in our sleep can lead to even more stress.

To tackle these issues, it's crucial to establish healthy boundaries with technology. A study published in the journal "Computers in Human Behavior" found that limiting the frequency of checking emails and social media led to lower stress and increased well-being among participants. By doing this, you regain control over your digital life and create space for other important activities.

Moreover, creating tech-free zones within your home can also be beneficial. The presence of digital devices in every corner of our homes can make it challenging to disconnect and relax. Research conducted by the Pew Research Center revealed that people who designate specific areas in their homes as tech-free zones tend to have better family relationships and a more peaceful atmosphere. This separation allows you to enjoy quality time with loved ones without the distractions of screens.

Another effective strategy to mitigate the stress caused by technology is to practice a digital detox. This means taking regular breaks from screens, whether it's your smartphone, computer, or television. By intentionally unplugging for a while, you can reduce information overload and recharge your mental batteries. This not only enhances your well-being but also boosts your productivity when you return to your digital tasks.

In addition to setting boundaries with technology, another crucial aspect of maintaining a healthy digital lifestyle is mindful consumption of digital content. This means being conscious of what you choose to engage with online. One practical step you can take is to unfollow accounts or platforms that consistently trigger stress or negative emotions. The constant exposure to distressing news or content can take a toll on your mental health. By curating your online feed to include more uplifting and informative content, you can create a more positive digital environment for yourself.

It's also essential to prioritize face-to-face interactions and outdoor activities. Spending quality time with friends and family in person has been shown to boost mood and reduce stress. And a study conducted by the University of Queensland found that spending at least 30 minutes in nature each week significantly lowers the risk of depression and high-stress levels. By balancing your digital exposure with real-world interactions and outdoor experiences, you can counteract the negative effects of excessive screen time.

While technology, social media, and the digital world offer many benefits, they can also significantly impact our stress levels. Information overload, social media comparison, and an "always-on" culture are some of the factors contributing to this stress. To combat these effects, it's crucial to establish boundaries, practice digital detox, and mindfully consume digital content. By taking these steps, we can better navigate the digital age while maintaining our mental well-being.

UNHEALTHY COPING MECHANISMS

Coping mechanisms are strategies that people use to deal with stress and difficult emotions. While some coping mechanisms can be healthy and effective, others can be quite unhealthy and potentially harmful. Unhealthy coping mechanisms are those that don't address the underlying issues causing stress and can even make the situation worse. Let's explore some of the most common unhealthy coping mechanisms.

One of the most common unhealthy coping mechanisms is avoidance. Avoidance refers to the act of ignoring or running away from whatever is causing you stress or discomfort. It's like pretending the issue doesn't exist or hoping it'll magically disappear. Many of us have done this at some point in our lives, thinking it might provide a quick escape from stress. However, avoidance may seem like a temporary relief, but it doesn't actually solve the problem.

Studies have shed light on this issue. For instance, there's a study published in the "Psychological Bulletin" that found avoidance to be counterproductive when it comes to dealing with stress. Instead of helping us, it tends to backfire over time. How? Well, when we avoid our problems, they don't just disappear; they tend to pile up and become even more stressful. This can lead to a vicious cycle of increasing stress and anxiety.

Imagine you're facing a challenging situation at work, and it's causing you a lot of stress. Instead of addressing it, you start avoiding your tasks, procrastinating, or even calling in sick to escape it. Initially, you might feel relieved, like you've dodged a bullet. But as time goes on, your work piles up, deadlines loom larger, and the stress intensifies. You'll likely end up feeling even more overwhelmed than before.

Avoidance can also negatively impact your mental health. It can lead to a constant state of anxiety because you're constantly dreading the unresolved issues you're avoiding. This anxiety can seep into other areas of your life, making it difficult to relax or enjoy anything fully.

So, while it might be tempting to avoid stressors, it's crucial to recognize that this isn't a healthy or effective coping mechanism. Instead, facing your stressors head-on, seeking support, and finding constructive ways to manage stress are much more beneficial in the long run.

Denial is like a close relative of avoidance, but it has its own distinct characteristics. When people use denial as a coping mechanism, they essentially refuse to acknowledge that a problem exists or downplay its significance. It's a way of shielding oneself from the harsh reality of a stressful situation, but unfortunately, it's not a healthy or effective way to deal with stress.

Imagine someone facing a significant issue, like a health problem or a troubled relationship. Instead of confronting the problem and seeking help or finding solutions, they convince themselves that there's no problem at all. They might say things like, "It's not that bad," or "I can handle it on my own." While this may temporarily provide a sense of relief or calm, it can lead to even more significant problems down the road.

Research and psychological studies have shown that denial as a coping mechanism can be detrimental. By refusing to acknowledge and address the source of stress, individuals miss out on opportunities to find healthier solutions and support systems. For instance, if someone denies a serious health issue, they might delay seeking medical attention, potentially worsening their condition.

Moreover, denial can prevent personal growth and self-improvement. When we deny our problems, we miss the chance to learn from them and develop valuable coping skills. Instead of growing and becoming more resilient, we remain stuck in a cycle of denial, which can lead to chronic stress and anxiety.

In essence, like avoidance, denial may provide temporary relief, but it's not a sustainable or beneficial way to cope with stress. It's crucial to recognize that facing reality, seeking help when needed, and finding healthier ways to manage stress are far more effective in the long run.

Another prevalent unhealthy coping mechanism for dealing with stress is substance use. This includes alcohol, drugs, or even excessive caffeine consumption. Many people turn to these substances to numb emotional pain and find solace, but it's important to understand that this approach is far from healthy or effective in the long run.

When individuals use substances like alcohol or drugs to cope with emotional pain or stress, they are essentially seeking a temporary escape from their feelings. It's like a way to numb themselves, at least temporarily, to the emotional turmoil they're experiencing. However, this numbing effect is short-lived, and it can lead to a host of negative consequences.

Research and studies have consistently shown that relying on substances to cope with stress can create a harmful cycle. Initially, the use of substances may provide a feeling of relief or relaxation, which can be seductive. But as tolerance builds, individuals often find themselves needing more of the substance to achieve the same numbing effect, leading to addiction and dependency.

Moreover, substances like alcohol and drugs can have severe physical and mental health consequences. Alcohol, for instance, can lead to addiction, liver damage, and a range of mental health issues. Illicit drugs can have even more devastating effects on both physical and mental well-being.

Excessive caffeine consumption may not be as severe as alcohol or drug abuse, but it can still lead to health problems like increased anxiety, disrupted sleep patterns, and heightened stress levels.

In the long term, relying on substances as a coping mechanism not only fails to address the root causes of stress but also creates new problems and exacerbates existing ones. It can strain relationships, hinder personal growth, and lead to a downward spiral of declining mental and physical health.

The next one is emotional eating. Emotional eating occurs when individuals use food as a means to cope with stress or negative emotions. While it might seem like a comforting way to soothe emotional distress, it often leads to weight gain and unhealthy eating habits.

Imagine a situation where you're feeling overwhelmed by stress, sadness, or frustration. In such moments, some people turn to their favorite comfort foods—maybe it's ice cream, pizza, or cookies—to find solace. This temporary relief is often followed by guilt or regret, as emotional eating rarely addresses the root causes of emotional distress.

Research published in the journal "Obesity" has shed light on the consequences of emotional eating. It has been found that emotional eating is strongly linked to obesity and poor emotional well-being. This is because, in times of emotional distress, individuals tend to consume more calories than they need, often choosing high-calorie, low-nutrient foods. This pattern of behavior can contribute to weight gain and health issues over time.

Furthermore, emotional eating can create a cycle of emotional distress. When individuals rely on food to cope with their emotions, they may not develop healthier strategies for managing stress or negative feelings. This can perpetuate a cycle where emotional eating leads to guilt, weight gain, and worsening emotional well-being, creating even more stress.

It's important to note that occasional indulgence in comfort foods is perfectly normal, but when it becomes a consistent pattern used as the primary way to cope with stress, it can have detrimental effects on physical and emotional health.

Another common way people cope with stress is by escaping into the world of social media.

In today's digital age, it's quite common for people to turn to their smartphones or computers when they're feeling stressed or overwhelmed.

Scrolling through social media feeds, watching videos, or engaging in online chats can provide a temporary escape from real-life problems. It's a way to disconnect from the stressors, if only for a short while.

However, the downside is that excessive social media use can become an unhealthy coping mechanism. Studies have consistently shown that spending too much time on social media can lead to increased feelings of anxiety and depression. This can happen for various reasons, including the pressure to compare oneself to others, exposure to negative news or comments, and the addictive nature of social media platforms that can lead to a sense of isolation and decreased self-esteem.

Moreover, excessive social media use can also interfere with other healthy coping strategies. Instead of addressing their stressors directly or seeking support from friends and family, individuals may find themselves constantly glued to their screens, which can further isolate them from meaningful real-world connections.

Another prevalent unhealthy coping mechanism is to channel all your energy into work as a means to escape personal stressors. While it might seem like a productive way to distract yourself from life's challenges, it often leads to burnout and a decline in overall well-being.

Imagine you're going through a tough time in your personal life, whether it's relationship problems, family issues, or health concerns. It's tempting to throw yourself into your work as a way to avoid dealing with these issues. Work can provide a sense of control and accomplishment, and it's a socially acceptable way to stay busy. However, over time, this approach can have detrimental consequences.

Research and studies have consistently shown that excessive workaholism can lead to burnout. Burnout is a state of physical and emotional exhaustion, often accompanied by reduced job performance. When you pour all your energy into work to escape personal problems, you're neglecting self-care and ignoring the need for emotional healing. This can result in decreased overall well-being and even further personal issues down the road.

Moreover, focusing solely on work can strain relationships and hinder personal growth. Neglecting personal issues can cause them to fester and worsen over time, making them even more challenging to address later.

And although there are others, the final unhealthy coping mechanism I want to mention is isolation. When individuals are stressed, they may sometimes resort to cutting off social connections and retreating into solitude as a way to cope. While occasional solitude can be beneficial for self-reflection and relaxation, chronic isolation can have negative effects, worsening feelings of loneliness and depression.

The COVID-19 lockdowns provided a stark example of the consequences of isolation. Many people experienced increased loneliness and depression during this period, as they were physically separated from their social circles for extended periods.

Research has shown that social connections are vital for mental and emotional well-being. Isolation can lead to a lack of emotional support, reduced opportunities for positive social interactions, and increased rumination on negative thoughts. This can exacerbate stress and emotional distress, making it challenging to cope effectively.

Unhealthy coping mechanisms may provide temporary relief from stress and difficult emotions, but they often result in negative long-term consequences for mental and physical health. It's important to recognize these behaviors and seek healthier alternatives, which is what we will discuss next.

CREATING A RELAXING ENVIRONMENT

Now that you have identified what you shouldn't do, let's go over some healthy ways to cope with stress, starting with your environment.

Creating a relaxing environment can be a game-changer when it comes to managing stress. Imagine your home or workspace as a haven of tranquility, where you can unwind and find peace amidst life's chaos. This simple change can work wonders for your mental well-being.

There are a bunch of things you can do to create a relaxing environment. Here are some suggestions.

The first one is to declutter your living space, and research supports this idea. A study published in the Personality and Social Psychology Bulletin discovered that people who lived in cluttered homes had higher levels of cortisol, which is a stress hormone, compared to those who had tidier living spaces. So, the first step in creating a relaxing environment is to declutter your surroundings.

When you declutter, you're not only clearing physical mess but also mental clutter. It allows your brain to focus better and feel less overwhelmed. You'll be able to find things more easily, which reduces frustration and stress.

Moreover, a clutter-free space can make you feel more in control and peaceful. It creates a sense of order and simplicity in your life, which can be comforting. So, by tidying up your living area, you're taking a concrete step towards reducing stress and promoting relaxation.

Reducing noise is another crucial element in creating a relaxing environment. Noise pollution can be quite bothersome and has the potential to trigger stress and even impact our health negatively. Research published in the journal Environmental Health Perspectives has shown a clear link between noise exposure and increased stress levels, as well as potential health issues such as heart disease.

When you minimize noise in your environment, you're essentially giving your mind a well-deserved break. Constant or loud noise can be mentally exhausting and make it difficult to relax. It can disrupt your concentration, sleep, and overall sense of calm. By creating a quieter space, you're helping your mind stay calm and reducing the stressors in your life.

Some ways to achieve this is by using noise-canceling headphones, soundproofing your home, or simply finding quieter areas to spend your time. You can also introduce soothing sounds like gentle music or nature sounds if they help you relax. The key is to create an environment that allows you to escape from the relentless noise of the outside world and find tranquility within your space.

On the flip side, music can be a powerful tool for relaxation. It has the ability to soothe our minds and reduce stress levels. One notable example is the song "Weightless" by Marconi Union, which has gained recognition for its stress-reducing qualities. In a study conducted by Mindlab International, it was found that listening to this particular song can lower anxiety levels by a remarkable 65%.

The calming effect of music like "Weightless" can be attributed to its composition, which includes a slow tempo, gentle melodies, and soothing sounds. Such music can have a profound impact on our emotional state and help us unwind after a long, stressful day.

However, it's important to note that everyone's musical preferences are unique. What works as a relaxation tool for one person may not have the same effect on another. So, while "Weightless" is a great choice for many, it's essential to explore different relaxing tunes and find the ones that resonate with your personal taste and bring you the most peace and tranquility.

Lighting also plays a vital role in creating a relaxing environment. Natural light, in particular, has a profoundly positive effect on our mood and well-being. Research has shown that exposure to natural light during the day can have several benefits, including improved sleep and reduced stress levels, especially in office workers.

Natural light helps regulate our body's internal clock, known as the circadian rhythm. This, in turn, can enhance the quality of our sleep, making it easier to fall asleep and wake up refreshed. It also promotes the production of serotonin, a neurotransmitter that contributes to feelings of well-being and happiness, helping to reduce stress.

To make the most of natural light, try to let it into your living or working spaces as much as possible. Open curtains or blinds during the day and position your workspace or relaxation area near windows. If you're in an environment with access to natural light, take advantage of it. It can make a noticeable difference in how you feel.

In contrast, harsh artificial lighting can be harsh on the eyes and contribute to feelings of discomfort and stress. So, whenever possible, opt for soft and warm artificial lighting. Soft, warm lighting, such as that from lamps with dimmer switches or candles, can create a cozy and calming atmosphere. This type of lighting is less harsh on the eyes and helps reduce the feeling of stress and tension. It's a simple way to transform a regular space into a tranquil oasis where you can unwind and destress.

When it comes to bedtime, dimming the lights is especially important. Our bodies have a natural circadian rhythm, which is like our internal body clock that regulates sleep and wake cycles. Bright or harsh lighting, especially in the evening, can disrupt this rhythm by signaling to our bodies that it's still daytime, making it harder to fall asleep.

Research has shown that exposure to bright or blue light in the evening can suppress the production of melatonin, a hormone that helps regulate sleep. This can lead to difficulty falling asleep and lower sleep quality. So, by dimming the lights in the evening, you're sending a signal to your body that it's time to relax and prepare for a restful night's sleep.

Plants can be wonderful stress-busters and have multiple benefits for your well-being. Indoor plants have been shown to help reduce stress and anxiety levels. The presence of greenery in your living or working space can create a sense of connection to the natural world, even when you're inside. This connection with nature is known to have a calming influence on our minds, helping us relax and feel more at ease.

Furthermore, indoor plants can improve air quality by absorbing carbon dioxide and releasing oxygen. They also filter out pollutants and toxins, creating a cleaner and healthier environment. Breathing in cleaner air can contribute to better overall health and a greater sense of well-being.

Taking care of plants can also be a therapeutic and stress-relieving activity in itself. It gives you a sense of responsibility and accomplishment as you watch your plants grow and thrive.

So, adding some green companions to your living or working space is not only aesthetically pleasing but also a practical way to reduce stress and create a more relaxing environment.

Color can also play a role in creating a relaxing environment. Blue and green hues are often associated with nature, water, and tranquility. Research suggests that these colors can help lower stress levels and create a serene atmosphere. When you surround yourself with shades of blue or green, whether through paint, decor, or even something as simple as colorful cushions, it can have a calming effect on your mind.

Using these colors strategically can also influence your mood positively. For example, soft blues and greens can make a space feel more peaceful, while deeper shades can add a sense of depth and coziness. The choice of color can be tailored to your personal preferences and the specific ambiance you want to create.

It's important to note that color perception can vary from person to person, so it's a good idea to choose shades that resonate with you personally and make you feel relaxed.

Next up, smell. Aromatherapy, which involves using essential oils to create pleasant scents, can work wonders for relaxation. Among the various essential oils, lavender stands out as a superstar when it comes to reducing stress and anxiety.

Lavender has been used for centuries to promote relaxation and alleviate tension. Research has shown that inhaling the scent of lavender can have a calming effect on the nervous system. One study published in the journal "Frontiers in Behavioral Neuroscience" in 2013 found that the aroma of lavender can decrease anxiety levels and improve mood.

The reason behind lavender's relaxation power lies in its ability to influence the limbic system, which is the part of our brain that controls emotions and stress responses. When you breathe in the soothing scent of lavender, it can trigger the release of certain neurotransmitters in the brain, like serotonin, which helps boost your mood and decrease stress.

You can use lavender essential oil in various ways to harness its stress-reducing benefits. One common method is to add a few drops of lavender oil to a diffuser and let it fill the air with its calming aroma. You can also dilute it in a carrier oil and apply it to your skin or add a few drops to a warm bath for a relaxing soak.

Taking a warm bath or shower can help you relax physically and mentally. First and foremost, a warm bath or shower can help relax your muscles. Warm water has a soothing effect on the body, and it can ease muscle tension and stiffness. Whether you've had a long day at work or a strenuous workout, immersing yourself in a warm bath or standing under a warm shower stream can provide almost instant relief. It's like giving your muscles a gentle massage, which can contribute to overall relaxation.

Beyond the physical benefits, warm baths and showers also have a calming effect on the mind. The sensation of warm water enveloping your body can be incredibly comforting. It's like a cozy embrace that helps melt away stress and anxiety. Many people find that taking a warm bath or shower is an excellent way to clear their minds and let go of the worries of the day.

Moreover, warm water can enhance your overall mood. It triggers the release of endorphins, which are natural mood elevators. As a result, you may experience a sense of contentment and relaxation while in the bath or shower and even after you've finished.

For an extra touch of relaxation, you can incorporate soothing scents, like lavender essential oil, which we discussed earlier, into your bath or shower routine. This combines the benefits of both warm water and aromatherapy for a more profound sense of relaxation.

Moving on from scents, you'll be amazed how just a breath of fresh air can help with stress reduction. When you open your windows or step outside, you allow yourself to connect with the natural environment. Fresh air carries with it not only oxygen but also a sense of rejuvenation and renewal. Breathing in clean, outdoor air can help clear your mind, reduce feelings of anxiety, and promote a sense of calmness.

Fresh air is particularly beneficial when you've been cooped up indoors for extended periods. It can serve as a refreshing break from the confines of indoor spaces and the potential build-up of indoor pollutants. Whether you take a leisurely walk in a park or simply open a window to let in a breeze, these moments of fresh air can contribute to improved mental well-being and stress relief.

Incorporating regular breaks for fresh air into your daily routine can be a simple yet effective strategy for managing stress and enhancing your overall sense of calm and contentment.

Lastly, personalization is key. Making your space uniquely your own by adding items that bring you joy and comfort can have a significant impact. This could include family photos, artwork, or sentimental objects that hold special meaning to you.

Having these reminders of happy moments and cherished memories in your living or working space can have several benefits. First, they can boost your mood by evoking positive emotions and creating a sense of nostalgia. When you glance at a favorite family photo or admire a piece of artwork that holds personal significance, it can bring a smile to your face and lighten your spirits.

Additionally, these personalized elements can provide emotional support during stressful times. When you're facing challenges or feeling overwhelmed, having a physical reminder of the people and moments that matter most to you can offer comfort and a sense of connection.

Personalization allows you to create a space that reflects your personality and values, making it a place where you feel truly at home. This sense of belonging and comfort can contribute to a relaxed and stress-free environment.

CREATING A SUPPORTIVE ENVIRONMENT

Having strong social connections is like having a natural stress-relief mechanism built into our lives. It's not just a nice-to-have; it's crucial for our well-being.

Research has shown that when we engage in positive social interactions with friends, family, or even coworkers, our bodies release oxytocin, a hormone often called the "love hormone" or "bonding hormone." Oxytocin helps reduce stress by lowering cortisol levels, which is the body's stress hormone. So, spending time with loved ones can literally help calm your nerves.

Furthermore, having a support system of friends and family can provide emotional comfort during challenging times. When you're facing stressors like work pressure, personal problems, or health issues, having someone to talk to and share your feelings with can make a world of difference. Studies have found that individuals with strong social support networks tend to experience lower levels of stress and are better equipped to cope with adversity.

Social connections also offer a sense of belonging and purpose, which can be powerful stress buffers. Feeling connected to others gives us a sense of meaning in our lives, and that can help us navigate through difficult situations more effectively. When you know you have people who care about you, it can boost your confidence and resilience in the face of stress.

Now, it's important to note that the quality of your social connections matters just as much as the quantity. Meaningful, positive relationships have a more significant impact on stress reduction than superficial ones. So, focus on nurturing those relationships that truly matter to you.

Don't underestimate the power of spending time with friends and loved ones when it comes to reducing stress. It's not just good for your mood; it's good for your overall well-being.

Here are some practical ways to build your support network.

First, stay connected with your existing friends and family. When you're feeling overwhelmed, just reaching out to a friend or a family member can make a world of difference. A study published in the journal "Psychological Bulletin" by Cohen and Wills in 1985 emphasized the importance of social support in coping with stress. They found that people with robust social networks are better equipped to handle life's challenges.

The beauty of staying connected is that it doesn't always require grand gestures. A simple call, text, or getting together for a cup of coffee can do wonders. Regular interaction helps you feel cared for and valued, which, in turn, reduces feelings of isolation and anxiety. A sense of belonging is a fundamental human need, and nurturing your existing relationships fulfills that need.

Moreover, when you stay in touch, you're not just receiving support; you're also providing it. Being there for your friends and family during their tough times fosters a sense of reciprocity and strengthens your bonds even further. It's a two-way street of support that can create a positive and stress-reducing cycle.

In essence, staying connected with your loved ones creates a warm and nurturing environment that plays a significant role in lowering stress. It's a simple yet powerful way to fortify your emotional well-being and build a robust support network.

For those of you that do not yet have a support network, or just want to expand your current one, there are a variety of ways to do it.

Engaging in clubs or groups that align with your interests can be a game-changer.

Being part of a group with common interests can boost your sense of belonging and reduce feelings of isolation, which is crucial for our mental well-being. When you feel like you belong, it helps alleviate stress and anxiety. Research published in the "Annals of Behavioral Medicine" by Hawkley and Cacioppo in 2010 underlines the significance of social connections in reducing loneliness and its negative impact on our health.

Moreover, these clubs or groups often offer a structured environment for social interaction. Whether it's a weekly meeting or a team event, it gives you a regular opportunity to connect with like-minded individuals. These interactions can lead to meaningful friendships, which can serve as a source of emotional support during stressful times.

What's particularly powerful about joining clubs or groups is that you're surrounded by people who share your interests. This common ground makes it easier to start conversations and build relationships. It's a more relaxed and natural way to connect with others compared to, say, networking events.

Social events, whether they're parties, gatherings, or other get-togethers, offer a valuable opportunity to broaden your social circle and, in turn, reduce stress. These occasions can be a lot more than just a good time; they're a chance to connect with new people and strengthen your existing relationships.

Research has found that participating in social activities is associated with increased happiness and well-being. A study published in the "Journal of Happiness Studies" in 2018 by Zawadzki et al. highlighted how socializing at events can enhance life satisfaction. Meeting new people and forming connections can provide a sense of fulfillment and purpose.

Moreover, social events often create a relaxed and enjoyable atmosphere, making it easier to strike up conversations and build connections. When you attend these gatherings, you're putting yourself in a situation where people are generally open to meeting others, which can ease any social anxiety you might have.

Expanding your social circle through social events can also be a valuable source of support. Having a diverse network of friends and acquaintances means you have a broader range of people to turn to when you need advice, comfort, or simply someone to talk to during stressful times.

Volunteering is a wonderful way to make a positive impact on your community and your own well-being. When you volunteer, you're not only doing good for others but also creating opportunities to connect with people who share your commitment to a cause. It's a win-win situation that can significantly contribute to reducing stress.

Studies have consistently shown that volunteering can have a profound impact on mental health. A review published in the "American Journal of Preventive Medicine" in 2013 by Anderson et al. highlighted that volunteering is associated with lower rates of depression and increased feelings of happiness. Engaging in meaningful activities like volunteering can boost your mood and reduce stress.

What's particularly special about volunteering is the sense of fulfillment it brings. When you dedicate your time and skills to a cause you care about, it can provide a deep sense of purpose and accomplishment. This feeling of making a positive difference in the world can be a powerful stress-reliever.

Moreover, volunteering often involves working alongside like-minded individuals who share your values and passions. These shared experiences can foster strong connections and friendships. When you volunteer together, you're part of a team that supports each other, creating a supportive and stress-reducing environment.

Another thing you can try out is to enroll in classes or workshops that align with your interests. These learning environments provide an excellent opportunity to connect with others who share your passion, and these learning settings often create a conducive atmosphere for social interaction.

When you're learning something new or improving a skill together with others, it's natural to strike up conversations and build connections. Common interests serve as an icebreaker, making it easier to form bonds.

What's great is that you're surrounded by individuals who have at least one shared interest with you. Whether it's a cooking class, a yoga session, or any other hobby or skill-based workshop, these shared experiences can lead to meaningful friendships.

Also, participating in classes or workshops is an avenue for personal growth and skill development. When you engage in activities you're genuinely interested in, it can boost your self-esteem and sense of accomplishment. This, in turn, can positively impact your overall well-being, reducing stress.

Professional relationships can also provide valuable support and opportunities that contribute to reducing stress.

Research has shown that having strong relationships with colleagues can lead to increased job satisfaction and reduced work-related stress. A study published in the "Journal of Applied Psychology" in 2017 by Liu et al. highlighted how positive workplace relationships can buffer the negative impact of job stress. Connecting with coworkers who understand your job-related challenges can be comforting and reassuring.

Furthermore, networking at work can open doors to career growth and development. When you build a network within your organization, you may discover new opportunities for collaboration, mentorship, or even career advancement. This sense of professional progress can positively influence your self-esteem and reduce stress associated with career concerns.

Moreover, your coworkers can provide emotional support during challenging times at work. Whether it's dealing with a difficult project, a tight deadline, or workplace changes, having a supportive network within your professional environment can make a significant difference in your ability to cope with stress.

If you find it challenging to build a support network due to issues like social anxiety or other personal challenges, seeking help from a therapist or counselor is a vital step toward improving your well-being and reducing stress.

Therapists and counselors are trained professionals who specialize in helping individuals overcome various emotional and psychological difficulties. They can provide you with the guidance and support you need to address the specific challenges that may be hindering your ability to build social connections.

Research has consistently shown that therapy can be highly effective in treating conditions like social anxiety disorder. For example, a study published in the journal "JAMA Psychiatry" in 2017 by Mayo-Wilson et al. found that cognitive-behavioral therapy (CBT) is an effective treatment for social anxiety disorder. CBT can help you identify and change negative thought patterns and behaviors that may be contributing to your social difficulties.

Therapists and counselors can also assist you in developing the necessary skills and strategies to build and maintain supportive relationships. They can help you build self-confidence, improve communication skills, and reduce anxiety in social situations.

Seeking professional help is a sign of strength, not weakness. It's a proactive step toward improving your mental health and overall quality of life. Remember that you don't have to navigate these challenges on your own.

Once you have your social network, taking the initiative to make plans or suggest activities is a proactive way to strengthen your relationships. When you initiate plans, you demonstrate to your friends and loved ones that you value the relationship. It sends a clear message that you care about spending time together and are willing to make an effort to maintain the connection. This kind of mutual effort in relationships can enhance trust and emotional bonds, reducing stress associated with feelings of neglect or isolation.

Being the one to initiate plans also allows you to have more control over the types of activities you engage in. You can choose activities that you find enjoyable and meaningful, which can further boost your mood and reduce stress. When you do things you love with people you care about, it creates positive experiences and lasting memories.

PHYSICAL ACTIVITY AND STRESS

Exercise is a great way to lower stress. When you get moving, like going for a jog or doing yoga, your brain releases chemicals called endorphins. These endorphins are like natural mood boosters, and they make you feel happier and less stressed.

Plus, exercise helps you blow off steam. When you're stressed, your body gets all tense, and your muscles get tight. But when you exercise, your muscles relax, and that can help reduce that feeling of stress. It's like a mini vacation for your body!

Another neat thing about exercise is that it can improve your sleep. When you're less stressed, you're more likely to sleep better, and better sleep means less stress. It's like a cycle of goodness!

Exercise also gives you a break from whatever is stressing you out. When you're working out, you're focused on your body and your movements, not your problems. It's like hitting the pause button on your stress, even if it's just for a little while.

And the best part is, you don't have to be a super athlete to reap the stress-reducing benefits of exercise. Even a simple walk around the block or some light stretching can help. So, no excuses!

When it comes to reducing stress through physical exercises, some types of workouts have been shown to be particularly effective.

First up, aerobic exercises like jogging, swimming, or cycling are fantastic for stress reduction. When you do aerobic exercise, it gets your heart pumping. Your body responds by releasing endorphins.

Also, like all types of exercise, when you're out there jogging or cycling, your mind gets a break from all the stressors in your life. The rhythmic movements and the steady breathing help clear your mind and reduce tension. So, it's not just your body that benefits; it's your headspace too.

Research published in the journal "Psychosomatic Medicine" has shown that regular aerobic exercise can help lower those stress hormones like cortisol and adrenaline. So, it's not just a feel-good theory; it's science telling us that aerobic exercises are legit stress reducers.

If you're someone who enjoys hitting the gym and lifting weights or doing resistance exercises, you're in for a double win – not only for your muscles but also for your stress levels.

A study published in the journal "JAMA Psychiatry" found that resistance training can significantly reduce symptoms of depression, which often goes hand in hand with stress.

When you engage in strength training, your body releases endorphins, those feel-good chemicals we talked about earlier. They not only make you feel happier but also help to take the edge off stress. Plus, when you see progress in your strength and physique, it can boost your self-esteem and confidence, making you better equipped to deal with life's challenges.

Next, we've got yoga. Yoga is your zen buddy when it comes to reducing stress. It's awesome because it blends physical movements with deep breathing and relaxation techniques. When you roll out that yoga mat and start flowing through poses, you're not just working on your flexibility and strength – you're also giving stress a run for its money.

The magic of yoga lies in its ability to help you become more in tune with your body and mind. As you move through different poses, you're encouraged to focus on your breath and stay present in the moment. This mindfulness aspect is like a secret weapon against stress. When you're aware of your body and your thoughts, you're better equipped to manage stress and anxiety.

Another great option is tai chi. Tai chi is like a graceful dance that's also a martial art – but don't worry, it's slow and gentle, not about throwing punches. This practice involves flowing movements that are as calming as they are beneficial for your body. Like yoga – Tai chi pairs these movements with deep, mindful breathing. It's like a beautiful blend of physical and mental well-being.

When you engage in these slow, flowing motions and synchronize them with your breath, it's like you're entering a moving meditation. This meditative quality helps you find your inner zen – that peaceful, stress-free state of mind.

Okay, that's it for this list of stress reducing exercises, but don't think these are your only choices. The truth is, all physical activity is good for lowering stress. The key is to find an activity you enjoy and can stick with – that's what will help you manage stress in the long run.

DIET AND NUTRITION

What you eat can have a big impact on how you feel. For example, when you eat a lot of sugary and highly processed foods, your blood sugar levels can go on a rollercoaster ride. This means you might feel a burst of energy followed by a crash, and that can make you feel more stressed out.

On the flip side, a balanced diet with plenty of fruits, vegetables, whole grains, and lean proteins can help keep your blood sugar stable. These foods provide a steady supply of energy, which can help you stay calm and focused. Research has also found that diets rich in antioxidants, like those found in fruits and veggies, may help reduce stress.

Let's get into some specific foods to help you beat stress, starting with leafy greens.

Leafy greens like spinach and kale are packed with magnesium, which can help reduce stress and anxiety. Studies have shown that people with higher magnesium levels tend to feel less stressed and anxious. Magnesium helps your body relax, both physically and mentally. It's like a natural chill pill!

When you're stressed, your body can actually use up more magnesium, so it's essential to keep those magnesium levels in check. Spinach and kale are awesome sources of this mineral. They help maintain that magnesium balance, which can help you feel more relaxed overall.

Next up, complex carbohydrates, particularly whole grains like brown rice, whole wheat pasta, and oats. These foods help your brain produce more serotonin which is like your brain's natural mood-lifter, a feel-good chemical. It's like giving your brain the tools to create its own happiness potion! Plus, these foods release energy slowly, so you don't get those energy crashes that can make you feel grumpy.

Protein is like the building blocks for your brain chemicals. It contains amino acids that your brain uses to create and balance its important chemicals. This balance is key in helping you manage stress and stay calm.

Lean proteins, such as chicken, turkey, and fish, are fantastic choices because they provide these amino acids without the extra saturated fats found in some other protein sources. They help your brain do its job effectively, which can reduce those stress levels.

Nuts and seeds, like almonds and pumpkin seeds, are like little stress-busting nuggets. They're packed with healthy fats and antioxidants that can help your body handle stress better. These nutrients work together to calm your nervous system and reduce those stress levels. Plus, they make for a convenient and tasty snack option!

Other seeds, like walnuts and flaxseeds, are also great sources of omega-3 fatty acids. Omega-3s have been linked to reducing stress and improving mood because they help lower inflammation in your body. Less inflammation means less stress on your system.

These healthy fats are also found in foods like salmon, avocados, and olive oil.

For those of you that need something sweet, dark chocolate, when savored in moderation, can be a sweet stress reliever.

Dark chocolate contains special compounds that have the power to relax your blood vessels and help reduce stress hormones in your body. When you're choosing your dark chocolate, look for options with at least 70% cocoa content. The higher cocoa content means more of those stress-busting compounds. So, a little square or two of high-cocoa dark chocolate can be a tasty and soothing way to de-stress.

But remember, moderation is the key here. Don't go overboard with the chocolate, or it might undo the stress-reducing benefits.

Herbal teas, like chamomile and green tea, are like warm hugs for your stress levels. They've been cherished for their calming properties for ages.

Chamomile tea is known for its ability to relax your muscles and calm your nerves. It contains compounds that bind to receptors in your brain, helping to reduce anxiety and promote relaxation.

Green tea is packed with antioxidants called catechins that have been linked to reduced stress. These little warriors help protect your cells from stress-related damage. Plus, the act of sipping on a warm cup of tea can be incredibly soothing in itself.

And finally, water. Hydration is like the unsung hero of stress management. It might seem simple, but not drinking enough water can actually make stress worse. When you're dehydrated, you can feel tired, cranky, and more irritable. These feelings can pile up and add to your stress levels.

On the flip side, staying well-hydrated is a secret weapon for resilience against stress. When you're hydrated, your body functions at its best. Your brain can think more clearly, your muscles work better, and your overall well-being gets a boost.

That's it for the stress-busting foods. Essentially, it is about eating a healthy balanced diet.

But before we move on, there are a couple of things to watch out for.

Caffeine, that beloved pick-me-up, can be a double-edged sword. While a cup of coffee can give you a little energy boost, too much caffeine can make you feel jittery and anxious. It can rev up your nervous system and make stress levels spike. So, it's best to enjoy your caffeine in moderation to avoid those jitters.

Also, alcohol. While it might seem like a way to unwind, excessive alcohol can actually disrupt your sleep. Poor sleep can make you feel even more stressed and irritable. So, it's essential to be mindful of your alcohol consumption, especially in the evening, if you want to wake up feeling refreshed and ready to take on the day.

TIME MANAGEMENT SKILLS

Good time management skills can be a game-changer when it comes to lowering stress. You see, life these days can get pretty hectic. Between work, personal responsibilities, and trying to find some relaxation time, it's easy to feel overwhelmed. But when you manage your time well, it can make a big difference in how you handle all these demands.

First off, let's talk about work. When you're good at managing your time at work, you're more likely to stay on top of your tasks and deadlines. This means you're less likely to feel rushed or pressured to complete things at the last minute. Studies have shown that this kind of proactive time management can reduce work-related stress. You feel more in control and less overwhelmed by your job.

Now, when you've got a handle on your work life, it frees up some precious time for your personal life. Balancing work and personal life can be a real challenge, but time management helps. You can allocate specific time for family, friends, and hobbies without feeling like you're neglecting any of them. This balance is essential for reducing overall stress levels because it ensures that you're not constantly burning the candle at both ends.

Speaking of personal life, relaxation time is crucial for stress reduction. When you manage your time effectively, you can set aside time for relaxation without feeling guilty. Studies have shown that activities like meditation, exercise, or simply unwinding with a book can significantly lower stress levels. When you're not constantly racing against the clock, you can truly enjoy these moments of relaxation.

Good time management skills help lower stress by allowing you to stay on top of work tasks, balance work and personal life, and make room for relaxation. It's about finding that sweet spot where you can juggle your responsibilities without feeling overwhelmed.

Now let's give you some specific strategies for effective time management.

First, prioritizing tasks. Prioritizing is like the compass that helps you navigate through your busy day. It means recognizing which tasks are most crucial and need your attention first.

Dr. Charles Duhigg, in his book "The Power of Habit," discusses the science behind habits and productivity. His research suggests that focusing on high-priority tasks can significantly boost your productivity. When you tackle important tasks first, you're more likely to make progress on your goals and feel a sense of accomplishment. This can boost your motivation and overall efficiency.

Imagine your day as a plate of different-sized dishes. Prioritizing is like placing the biggest and most important dishes on your plate first. This ensures you're dealing with the critical stuff before you fill up on less important tasks. It's a simple concept, but it can make a big difference.

But how do you determine what's most important? One approach is to consider the consequences of not doing a task. If not doing it will have a significant impact, it's likely a high-priority task. Also, think about your long-term goals. Tasks that align with your goals are often high-priority.

In a study by Locke and Latham, published in the journal "Current Directions in Psychological Science," they emphasize the importance of setting clear goals. Prioritizing is closely linked to goal-setting. When you prioritize tasks that are aligned with your goals, you're not only managing your time effectively but also working towards what truly matters to you.

Prioritizing your tasks means identifying and tackling the most important ones first. It's not just about being productive; it's about making meaningful progress towards your goals.

Let's dive a little deeper on goal setting. Setting clear goals is like drawing a roadmap for your life and work, helping you stay on track and motivated.

The idea behind setting clear goals is pretty straightforward: if you don't know where you're going, it's challenging to get there efficiently. This concept goes hand in hand with time management because having well-defined goals can make it easier to prioritize your tasks and manage your time effectively.

A study published in the American Journal of Lifestyle Medicine highlights the positive impact of goal setting on time management and motivation. When you clearly define your goals, you create a sense of purpose and direction. This can be a powerful motivator. It's like having a destination in mind when you embark on a journey; it gives your efforts meaning and direction.

Moreover, setting clear goals allows you to break down big tasks into smaller, manageable steps. This is particularly useful for time management. You can allocate specific time blocks to work on these smaller tasks, making it easier to achieve your larger goals over time.

Think of goal setting as the foundation of your time management strategy. It's the starting point that guides your decisions about what tasks to prioritize and how to allocate your time effectively. Without clear goals, you might find yourself drifting aimlessly through your day, which can lead to inefficiency and stress.

Whether it's a career goal, a personal goal, or a project goal, taking the time to clearly define your objectives can significantly improve your ability to manage your time effectively and stay motivated.

Making a to-do list might sound simple, but it's another powerful tool that can help you stay organized, reduce stress, and improve your focus.

Imagine your mind as a cluttered room, filled with all the tasks, responsibilities, and ideas you need to keep track of. When you create a to-do list, it's like tidying up that room and putting everything in its place. This simple act can provide a sense of order and clarity.

A study published in the journal Psychological Science supports the idea that writing down tasks can have a positive impact on mental clarity and focus. When you jot down what you need to accomplish, it's as if you're offloading those thoughts from your mind onto paper.

This frees up mental space, reduces the mental clutter, and allows you to concentrate better on the task at hand.

Moreover, a to-do list serves as a visual reminder of what needs to be done. It keeps your tasks in front of you, preventing things from slipping through the cracks. This can reduce the anxiety that often comes from trying to remember everything.

Creating a to-do list also helps with prioritization, which we've discussed earlier. Once you have your tasks listed, you can decide which ones are most important and need your immediate attention. This is a key aspect of effective time management because it ensures that you're focusing on what matters most.

In essence, making a to-do list is like creating a roadmap for your day. It helps you stay organized, reduces mental clutter, improves your focus, and ensures that you're managing your time effectively. So, whether you prefer a digital app or a good old-fashioned pen and paper, this simple practice can make a big difference in your productivity and stress levels.

Next, let's explore the concept of using time blocks. This technique is like having a structured schedule that can boost your productivity and focus.

The idea behind using time blocks is to break your workday into manageable chunks. One well-known method that uses time blocks is the Pomodoro Technique, which was developed and studied by Francesco Cirillo. In this technique, you work for a focused 25-minute period, called a "Pomodoro," followed by a short 5-minute break. After completing four Pomodoros, you take a longer break, typically around 15-30 minutes.

Francesco Cirillo's research and practice have shown that this time-blocking approach can enhance productivity. It capitalizes on the brain's ability to stay engaged and alert for a limited period, preventing burnout or mental fatigue that can occur during long, uninterrupted work sessions.

Using time blocks helps you allocate specific periods for different tasks. This structured approach ensures that you're dedicating focused attention to your work. It's like dividing your day into compartments, each with its specific purpose, which can make your workflow smoother and more efficient.

Additionally, time blocking encourages you to set clear boundaries between work and breaks. This can be essential for maintaining a healthy work-life balance, as it prevents you from overworking yourself. The structured breaks also provide opportunities to recharge, which can improve overall productivity and reduce stress.

Using time blocks is a valuable time management strategy. It promotes focused work, prevents burnout, and allows for regular breaks, enhancing both productivity and well-being.

Now to dispel a common myth: multitasking. While multitasking might seem like a way to get more done, research in the Journal of Experimental Psychology suggests otherwise.

Multitasking involves juggling multiple tasks simultaneously. It's like trying to spin multiple plates at once. The research findings indicate that multitasking can lead to reduced efficiency. It might seem like you're accomplishing more, but in reality, you're often switching your focus rapidly between tasks, and this can lead to mistakes, decreased productivity, and increased stress.

When you focus on one task at a time, you're giving it your full attention. This dedicated focus can lead to better concentration and higher-quality work. It's like giving each task its own spotlight instead of trying to share the stage with others.

Moreover, focusing on one task at a time can lead to a sense of accomplishment. When you complete a task without distractions, you're more likely to feel a sense of closure, which can be rewarding and boost your motivation to tackle the next task.

Avoiding multitasking also helps with time management because it allows you to allocate specific time blocks for each task. You can prioritize what's most important and give it your full attention, ensuring that you're using your time efficiently.

Now let's explore the significance of learning to say no. It's like creating a protective shield around your time and mental energy.

Imagine your time and energy as finite resources, much like a limited budget. When you say yes to every request or commitment that comes your way, it's as if you're overspending that budget. Overcommitting can lead to stress because you spread yourself too thin, and you may struggle to meet all your obligations effectively.

A study in the Journal of Personality and Social Psychology highlights the positive impact of setting boundaries, which includes learning to say no when necessary. Setting boundaries is like establishing healthy limits around your time and energy. When you do this, you're safeguarding your well-being.

Learning to say no allows you to prioritize what truly matters to you. It's about recognizing your own limits and commitments and respecting them. By doing so, you can focus on tasks and activities that align with your goals and values, reducing the stress that can come from trying to do it all.

Moreover, saying no can be a form of self-care. It's about valuing your own well-being and ensuring that you have the time and energy to take care of yourself. When you're not constantly overextending yourself, you have a better chance of maintaining a healthy work-life balance and reducing the risk of burnout.

Saying no helps you allocate your time more effectively to what truly matters. It ensures that you have the necessary time and resources to excel in your commitments and prevents you from spreading yourself too thin.

For you saying no to getting others to say yes: delegation. Delegation is like sharing the workload and making the most of your team's abilities.

Imagine you're the captain of a ship. Instead of trying to do everything yourself, delegation is like having a reliable crew you can trust to handle specific tasks. When you delegate, you're not only making the best use of your team's skills but also freeing up your own time and mental energy.

A study featured in the Harvard Business Review underscores the positive impact of delegation. When you pass on tasks to others, it can significantly free up your time. You're not bogged down by every little detail, which can lead to reduced stress. Delegation allows you to focus on higher-level responsibilities and strategic thinking.

Delegating also encourages collaboration and teamwork. When you involve others in the process, it can lead to more innovative solutions and better outcomes. It's like tapping into a collective pool of knowledge and expertise.

Moreover, delegation can be a key factor in work-life balance. When you're able to entrust tasks to your team or colleagues, you're less likely to carry the weight of the entire workload on your shoulders. This can help you maintain a healthier work-life balance, reducing the risk of burnout and stress.

Delegation ensures that tasks are distributed efficiently, and the right people are handling them. It's about playing to each team member's strengths, which can improve overall productivity.

Now let's move away from people to technology, because in today's digital age, technology can be both a powerful ally and a potential distraction.

Using technology wisely is like having a toolbox filled with helpful gadgets. Productivity apps and tools can streamline your tasks, improve organization, and ultimately, enhance your time management skills.

Research published in the journal Cyberpsychology, Behavior, and Social Networking emphasizes the value of using technology mindfully to boost productivity. Mindful use of technology means harnessing its capabilities without falling into the trap of constant distraction.

Productivity apps can help you create to-do lists, set reminders, and manage your calendar efficiently. They serve as digital assistants, ensuring you stay on track with your tasks and appointments. It's like having a personal organizer at your fingertips.

However, it's essential to strike a balance. While technology can aid time management, overuse or misuse can lead to reduced productivity. The key is to use technology intentionally and avoid unnecessary distractions, like excessive social media scrolling or email checking.

Moreover, technology offers flexibility in how and where you work. Remote collaboration tools, for instance, can enable efficient teamwork, allowing team members to work together seamlessly from different locations. It's like having a virtual office that adapts to your needs.

Using technology wisely means optimizing your digital tools to work for you, not against you. It's about finding the right apps and strategies that align with your goals and daily routines.

Once you have chosen your time management strategies, it is necessary to regularly review and adjust them. This practice is like fine-tuning your car to ensure it runs smoothly, but for your productivity and effectiveness.

Life is dynamic, and what works well for your time management today may not be as effective tomorrow. That's where the "Review and Adjust" process comes into play. It's about taking a step back, evaluating your strategies, and making necessary tweaks to stay on track.

David Allen, in his book "Getting Things Done," popularized the "Weekly Review" technique. This approach involves setting aside a specific time each week to reflect on your goals, tasks, and priorities. It's like having a regular check-in with yourself to see how you're progressing.

The "Weekly Review" technique encourages you to ask important questions: Are you making progress toward your goals? Are there tasks that are consistently causing delays or stress? Are there new priorities or opportunities that have arisen?

Regularly assessing your time management strategies can help you identify areas for improvement. Maybe you've noticed that a particular task always takes longer than expected. By recognizing this, you can adjust your time allocation or find ways to streamline the task.

Moreover, life can throw unexpected curveballs your way. The "Review and Adjust" process ensures that you can adapt to changing circumstances. It's like having a backup plan ready when things don't go as planned.

This practice is essential for maintaining efficiency and reducing stress. By proactively identifying and addressing issues, you can prevent small problems from turning into significant setbacks.

Finally, don't overlook the significance of taking breaks and resting. It's like recharging your energy to keep your productivity engine running smoothly.

In a fast-paced world, it's easy to believe that constant work and hustle lead to greater productivity. However, research published in the Journal of Organizational Behavior and Human Decision Processes highlights the importance of taking breaks.

Imagine your mind as a computer. Just like a computer, it needs regular breaks to cool down and function optimally. When you take breaks, you're allowing your brain to recharge and reset. It's like stepping away from a task to catch your breath before diving back in.

These breaks can improve your focus and creativity. When you return to work after a break, you're often more refreshed and better equipped to tackle challenges. It's like pressing the reset button on your mental clarity and problem-solving abilities.

Moreover, taking breaks can prevent burnout and reduce stress. Overworking without breaks can lead to exhaustion, reduced productivity, and increased stress levels. On the other hand, planned breaks give you a chance to recuperate, which can help you maintain a healthy work-life balance.

Incorporating regular breaks into your schedule can enhance overall productivity. Short breaks, much like using time blocks, can be used to clear your mind, stretch, or take a quick walk. These moments of rest can improve your efficiency and prevent mental fatigue, which can slow you down.

The key is to strike a balance between work and rest. Recognize that taking breaks is not a waste of time but an investment in your productivity and well-being. Whether it's a short break during the day or a longer rest period between tasks, it's an essential part of effective time management.

BREATHING EXERCISES

Breathing exercises are simple techniques that help you control your breath in specific ways to promote relaxation and reduce stress. They're like little tricks to help you take a breather, quite literally! These exercises focus on the way you inhale and exhale, and they can be done just about anywhere, whether you're at home, work, or even stuck in traffic.

Now, why are they so good for stress reduction? Well, it all comes down to how our bodies react to stress. When we're stressed, our bodies tend to take shallow, quick breaths, which can make us feel even more anxious. Breathing exercises work by encouraging deep, slow breaths. When you take slow, deep breaths, it activates your body's relaxation response.

Studies have shown that practicing deep breathing can lower your heart rate and blood pressure, which are both indicators of stress. It also reduces the levels of stress hormones in your body. One study published in the "Journal of Alternative and Complementary Medicine" found that deep breathing exercises significantly reduced anxiety and stress levels in participants.

Another reason breathing exercises are so effective is that they can be a mindful practice. Mindfulness is all about being present in the moment, and focusing on your breath is a great way to do that. When you concentrate on your breath, you naturally let go of other worries and thoughts that may be causing you stress.

Breathing exercises are a simple but powerful tool for stress reduction. They can help you calm your mind, lower your heart rate, and decrease stress hormone levels in your body. Plus, they're easy to do and can be a quick fix in stressful situations.

Here are a few simple breathing exercises you can try out the next time you feel stressed. Give each on a go and then use the one that works best for you.

The first one is the physiological sigh. It involves taking two deep breaths through your nose and then exhaling slowly through your mouth. The first nasal breath fills your lungs almost to capacity, and the second quick inhale further opens up your air sacs.

Our normal breathing pattern often becomes shallow, especially when we're stressed or anxious. We tend to take quick, shallow breaths, which can lead to insufficient oxygen exchange in our lungs. This shallow breathing can actually signal to our body that we're in a state of stress or danger, triggering the release of stress hormones like cortisol.

The physiological sigh works by interrupting this shallow breathing pattern. When you take the first deep breath through your nose, you're filling your lungs almost to their maximum capacity. This allows more oxygen to enter your bloodstream, which is important because oxygen is essential for your body to function properly.

The second quick nasal inhale that follows further opens up the air sacs in your lungs. These little air sacs, called alveoli, are where oxygen and carbon dioxide are exchanged. By taking that quick second breath, you ensure that more of your alveoli get involved in the exchange process, allowing for even better oxygenation of your blood.

Exhaling slowly through your mouth after these two deep inhales helps release any stale air and carbon dioxide from your lungs. It also encourages you to expel tension and stress along with the breath.

By practicing the physiological sigh, you're essentially resetting your breathing pattern from shallow and stressed to deep and relaxed. You flood your body with fresh oxygen, calm your nervous system, and send signals to your brain that it's time to relax. It's a quick and effective way to promote relaxation and reduce stress in just a few breaths.

The second technique is called "box breathing." It's pretty simple. You start by inhaling slowly through your nose for a count of four seconds, then hold your breath for another four seconds. After that, exhale slowly through your mouth for another four seconds, and finally, wait for four seconds before starting the next cycle.

Your body has two parts of the nervous system: the sympathetic and the parasympathetic. The sympathetic nervous system is like the gas pedal in a car; it revs you up and prepares you for action when you're stressed. On the other hand, the parasympathetic nervous system is like the brakes; it helps you relax and calm down.

Now, box breathing is like hitting the brakes. When you inhale slowly through your nose for four seconds, hold your breath for another four seconds, exhale slowly through your mouth for four seconds, and then pause for four seconds before starting the next cycle, you're creating a balanced, rhythmic pattern. This balanced pattern signals to your body that it's time to slow down, triggering the parasympathetic nervous system. It's like saying, "Hey, it's okay, no need to be stressed right now."

By doing this, you reduce the release of stress hormones like cortisol. These hormones are like the alarm bells in your body when you're stressed, and box breathing helps lower their volume. When the stress hormones decrease, you feel calmer and more relaxed.

Box breathing also gives your mind something to focus on – the counting and the rhythm. This mindfulness aspect helps clear your head of racing thoughts and worries, which are often big contributors to stress. It's like hitting the reset button for your mind, allowing you to think more clearly and calmly.

Moreover, this technique maintains a balance between oxygen and carbon dioxide in your bloodstream. When you inhale and exhale for four seconds each, it ensures a consistent exchange of these gasses in your lungs. This balance is vital for your overall well-being and can further contribute to stress reduction.

The last technique is called diaphragmatic breathing. This one's all about using your diaphragm, which is a muscle located just below your lungs. To do it, sit or lie down comfortably and place one hand on your chest and the other on your belly. Take a slow, deep breath through your nose, letting your belly rise as you fill your lungs. Then, exhale slowly through your mouth, feeling your belly fall.

When you take a slow, deep breath through your nose while allowing your belly to rise as you fill your lungs, you're engaging your diaphragm. This deep inhalation draws in more air, and that's important because oxygen is like fuel for your body. It's needed for your cells to function properly.

The exhalation part is equally important. When you exhale slowly through your mouth and feel your belly fall, you're ensuring a complete exchange of air in your lungs. This means that you're not just taking in more oxygen, but you're also expelling more carbon dioxide, which is a waste product that can build up when you're stressed.

This type of breathing helps your body enter a state of relaxation. When you breathe deeply and engage your diaphragm, you send signals to your brain that everything is okay, and there's no need for the "fight or flight" response associated with stress.

Studies have shown that diaphragmatic breathing can lower your heart rate and blood pressure, both of which are indicators of stress. It also reduces the levels of stress hormones in your body. So, it's not just a physical sensation; it's a physiological response that promotes relaxation and stress reduction.

PROGRESSIVE MUSCLE RELAXATION

Progressive muscle relaxation (PMR) is a straightforward and potent technique that can work wonders in reducing stress and muscle tension. Think of it as a little gift you give your body, a sort of mini-vacation that allows you to unwind and recharge. The beauty of PMR lies in its simplicity – you don't need any special equipment or skills to get started. All you need is a bit of time and a quiet place to practice.

Research has delved into the effectiveness of PMR, and the results are quite encouraging. It's not just a feel-good exercise; it has practical benefits. Numerous studies have shown that regular practice of PMR can help people manage anxiety, cope with insomnia, and improve their overall sense of well-being.

When you engage in PMR, you're essentially taking a journey through your own body, starting from your toes and gradually working your way up to your head. Along the way, you deliberately tense each muscle group for a short period – usually around 5-10 seconds – and then consciously release that tension. It's this contrast between tension and relaxation that makes PMR so effective.

The process isn't rushed; in fact, it encourages you to slow down and reconnect with your body. As you tense and then release each muscle group, you become more aware of the physical sensations and how tension feels compared to relaxation. This heightened awareness can be a powerful tool for managing stress because it allows you to recognize and address tension in your body as it arises.

One of the key benefits of PMR is that it teaches your body how to relax. Over time, as you practice regularly, your muscles become more adept at letting go of tension on their own. This means that when you encounter stressful situations in your daily life, you're better equipped to remain calm and avoid the physical buildup of stress in your body.

In a world where stress and tension often seem like constant companions, PMR offers a simple yet effective way to take control and find some peace amidst the chaos. It's not just a technique; it's a valuable tool for improving your mental and physical well-being.

To do PMR, first find a quiet and comfortable place where you won't be disturbed. You can sit or lie down, whatever feels best for you.

Start with deep breathing. Take a few deep breaths to calm your mind. Inhale slowly through your nose for a count of four, hold for a count of four, and then exhale through your mouth for a count of four. Do this a few times to settle in.

When you are ready, focus your attention on your toes. Tense the muscles in your toes and hold for 5 seconds. You should feel the tension but not to the point of pain. Then, release and let go. Feel the relaxation as the tension melts away.

Move on to the next muscle group, usually your feet or calf muscles. Tense them, hold, and then release. Gradually work your way up through your legs, thighs, abdomen, chest, arms, and neck. Tense each muscle group for 5 seconds and then release.

As you go through each muscle group, keep breathing steadily. Inhale as you tense the muscles, and exhale as you release. This helps you stay relaxed.

Pay attention to the difference between the tension and relaxation in each muscle group. This contrast is what makes PMR effective.

Remember, take your time and go at your own pace. It's not a race. Spend a few moments with each muscle group.

Finish with your face and head. Tense your facial muscles by scrunching up your face, then release. Finally, tense the muscles in your neck and shoulders, and then let go.

After you've gone through all the muscle groups, take a few deep breaths and enjoy the overall feeling of relaxation in your body.

The more you practice PMR, the better you'll become at recognizing and releasing tension in your body. Aim for daily sessions or whenever you feel stressed.

Progressive muscle relaxation can be a great tool to help you unwind and manage stress. Remember, it might take some practice to get the hang of it, but over time, it can become a valuable part of your stress management routine.

MINDFULNESS AND MEDITATION

When we're stressed, our bodies go into "fight or flight" mode. That's our natural response to danger, but these days, it can happen even when there's no real threat. Mindfulness and meditation help calm down this response. Studies have shown that regular meditation can lower the levels of stress hormones like cortisol in our bodies. So, it's like hitting the "chill" button for your brain.

Mindfulness is all about paying attention to the present moment without judgment. When we practice mindfulness, we're not dwelling on past regrets or worrying about the future. This can break the cycle of stress because a lot of it comes from thinking about what's already happened or what might happen next.

Imagine your mind as a constantly churning river of thoughts. Many of these thoughts revolve around what's already happened (the past) or what might happen (the future). When we dwell on past regrets, we're essentially reliving those moments, often accompanied by feelings of guilt, sadness, or anger. Similarly, when we worry about the future, we're creating scenarios in our minds, often negative ones, which can trigger anxiety and fear.

When you practice mindfulness, you're intentionally redirecting your focus away from the past and future and bringing it to the present moment. It's like stepping out of the turbulent river of thoughts and onto the peaceful riverbank.

By doing this, you're not denying the importance of your past experiences or the need to plan for the future. Instead, you're learning to observe these thoughts without judgment. You're not labeling them as good or bad; you're simply acknowledging their existence. This non-judgmental awareness is a key aspect of mindfulness.

Now, why does this matter for stress? Well, much of our stress comes from the stories we tell ourselves about the past and future. We might dwell on past mistakes, thinking we're not good enough, or we might fret about future challenges, fearing failure. These thought patterns can trigger the body's stress response, even though the events are not happening right now.

Mindfulness helps break this cycle because it interrupts the automatic reaction to these thoughts. Instead of getting swept away by them, you're observing them from a distance. This creates a mental space where you can choose how to respond. You might realize that those past regrets no longer define you, or you might recognize that the future is uncertain, and worrying won't change that.

Mindfulness is like a mental shift from time-traveling through regrets and worries to anchoring yourself in the here and now, offering respite from the cycle of stress-inducing thoughts and emotions.

Meditation, on the other hand, is like a workout for your mind. It helps you become more aware of your thoughts and feelings. When you meditate, you're training your brain to stay calm and focused, even when things get hectic. This means you're less likely to get swept away by stressful thoughts and emotions.

Think of meditation as a mental gym session. Just as physical exercise strengthens your body, meditation is a way to strengthen your mind. It's like lifting weights for your inner awareness. When you meditate, you're intentionally setting aside time to practice being present and attentive to your thoughts and feelings.

During meditation, you're encouraged to focus on a specific point of attention, like your breath or a mantra. This concentration exercise is like using a mental "anchor" to keep your thoughts from drifting into stressful territory. When your mind inevitably wanders (as minds tend to do), meditation teaches you not to react but to gently guide your attention back to that anchor.

As you continue to practice meditation, you're essentially flexing your "attention muscle." This helps you become more skilled at staying calm and focused, even in the face of life's chaos. Stressful thoughts and emotions may still arise, but you're less likely to get swept away by them because you've built up this mental strength and self-awareness.

Studies, such as those published in the "Journal of Alternative and Complementary Medicine" and "Psychoneuroendocrinology," have shown that meditation can have a positive impact on reducing stress and anxiety. It's like giving your mind the tools it needs to navigate the challenges of life with greater composure and resilience.

Meditation is a way to build inner strength and resilience, making it less likely that stress will push you around. Just as you wouldn't expect to run a marathon without training, meditation helps prepare your mind for the marathon of daily life, enabling you to stay calm and focused even when things get hectic.

Now that you know a bit of the background of mindfulness and meditation, let's give you some tools.

The first is a body scan. This is also known as **NDSR** or Yoga Nidra. This is a simple yet powerful way to become more in tune with your body and reduce stress.

To start, find a comfortable place to either lie down or sit. Make sure you won't be disturbed for a few minutes. Close your eyes if you like, and take a few deep breaths to settle in. Now, mentally start scanning your body from the top of your head all the way down to your toes. Pay close attention to each area, and notice if there are any places where you feel tension or discomfort.

As you move through each part of your body, try to release any tension you find. Imagine sending your breath and relaxation to those areas. This practice helps you become aware of physical stress that you might not have noticed otherwise. It's like giving your body a little tune-up, allowing you to let go of tension and relax more deeply.

The next technique is mindful walking. Begin by taking a leisurely walk in a place where you feel comfortable and safe. It could be a park, a quiet street, or any area you prefer. As you walk, pay close attention to each step you take. Feel the sensation of your feet making contact with the ground. Notice how the ground feels beneath your feet—whether it's soft grass, a paved path, or something else.

Notice your other senses also. What you smell, see, hear, and even how the air tastes. Immerse yourself in the present moment, focusing solely on your walking experience.

We've already given you some breathing exercises, but this one is a bit more on the meditation side. It's called breath counting.

Find a quiet and comfortable place to sit. It could be a chair or cushion, as long as you can sit with your back straight and your hands resting comfortably. Close your eyes gently if you like, or keep them softly focused on a spot in front of you.

Now, start counting your breaths from one to ten. As you inhale, silently say "one" to yourself, and as you exhale, say "two." Continue counting each breath in this way, up to ten. After you reach ten, start over from one.

The key to this practice is to stay focused on your breath and the counting. If your mind starts to wander, as it often does, don't worry or get frustrated. Simply acknowledge the distraction and gently bring your attention back to counting your breaths.

This practice may seem simple, but it's a form of meditation that can help train your mind to stay present and reduce stress. It encourages mindfulness and concentration, which can lead to a greater sense of calm and clarity.

Another breathing meditation is breath awareness. This is a straightforward and calming mindfulness practice.

Find a quiet and comfortable place to sit or lie down. You don't need any special equipment or position for this practice. Close your eyes if you prefer or keep them softly focused on a point in front of you.

Now, simply observe your breath without trying to change it in any way. Pay attention to the natural rhythm of your breath—the rise and fall of your chest or abdomen, or the sensation of air passing through your nostrils. Notice the gentle flow of your breath as it comes and goes.

Your mind may wander, and that's perfectly normal. When it does, gently redirect your focus back to your breath. You don't need to judge or criticize yourself for any distractions. Like all mindfulness meditations, the goal is to be aware of your breath and the present moment.

A classic ancient Buddhist meditation is Loving-kindness meditation, also known as Metta meditation. This is a heartwarming practice that can enhance feelings of well-being and reduce stress.

Begin by finding a comfortable and quiet place to sit or lie down. Close your eyes gently if you like, and take a few deep breaths to settle in.

Silently send yourself heartfelt wishes for happiness, health, and peace. You might say something like, "May I be happy. May I be healthy. May I live in peace."

Continue to send these loving wishes to yourself for a few moments, allowing the warmth of your feelings to grow. Then, gradually extend those wishes to include someone you genuinely care about, like a friend, family member, or loved one. Imagine them in your mind and silently send them heartfelt wishes for happiness, health, and peace. Say, "May you be happy. May you be healthy. May you live in peace."

Next, expand your circle of well-wishing to include others in your life, such as acquaintances, coworkers, and even people you may have conflicts with. Say, "May they be happy. May they be healthy. May they live in peace."

Studies published in the "Journal of Happiness Studies" have shown that practicing loving-kindness meditation can have positive effects on your well-being. It can boost feelings of happiness, compassion, and reduce stress and negative emotions.

This meditation cultivates a sense of love, compassion, and goodwill toward yourself and others, promoting a positive and serene state of mind. It's a wonderful practice to foster kindness and reduce stress in your life.

One of my favorite meditations is sound awareness. Close your eyes and just pay attention to all the sounds.

Start by paying attention to the sounds around you. Listen to everything—sounds that are close, like the hum of appliances or the ticking of a clock, and sounds that are far, like distant traffic or voices. Notice the difference between man-made sounds, such as cars passing by or construction work, and natural sounds, like the wind rustling through the trees or birds chirping.

Allow yourself to immerse in the auditory world around you. Try not to judge or label the sounds, but simply observe them as they come and go. If your mind starts to wander, gently bring your focus back to the sounds you hear.

This practice of active listening can be incredibly calming and grounding. It helps you connect with the present moment and become more aware of your surroundings. It's a way to appreciate the richness of the world through your sense of hearing.

Finally, guided meditation. Guided meditation involves listening to recordings or using meditation apps that provide step-by-step instructions and relaxation exercises. These recordings are typically led by experienced meditation instructors or therapists. They guide you through the entire meditation process, making it easy for beginners and experienced meditators alike.

You can find thousands of guided meditations online for free covering most of the exercises we have discussed here. The instructions can help you stay with the meditation, reducing wandering of the mind. They often also come with a soothing voice and calming music or sounds in the background create a serene atmosphere, making it easier to relax and unwind.

Or if you want a more personalized experience with a qualified teacher, you can try Transcendental Meditation. Search it online to find a local teacher.

Remember, practicing these exercises regularly can be more effective in lowering stress. You can start with just a few minutes a day and gradually increase the time as you become more comfortable with the practices.

COGNITIVE BEHAVIORAL TECHNIQUES

Cognitive Behavioral Techniques, often called CBT for short, are a set of strategies used to help people better understand and manage their thoughts, feelings, and behaviors. CBT is a widely used approach in psychology and therapy because it's effective for a variety of issues like anxiety, depression, stress, and even phobias.

CBT is based on the idea that our thoughts, feelings, and behaviors are interconnected. It's like a cycle. For example, if you constantly think negative thoughts, it can make you feel bad, and that, in turn, can lead to unhelpful behaviors. CBT helps break this cycle by teaching you to identify and change those negative thought patterns.

Studies have shown that CBT is effective because it's practical and focused on the here and now. It helps you develop coping skills to deal with life's challenges. One study published in the Journal of Consulting and Clinical Psychology found that CBT is especially effective for treating anxiety disorders.

CBT is a collaborative approach, which means you work closely with a trained therapist. They help you recognize your automatic negative thoughts and challenge them. It's like having a coach who guides you toward more positive and constructive thinking.

Another study in the journal JAMA Psychiatry found that CBT can be as effective as medication for treating depression, and the benefits can last longer. It gives you tools to manage your mood and prevent relapses.

Cognitive Behavioral Techniques are also helpful for reducing stress through a method called cognitive restructuring. It's like a mental makeover that helps you change your stressful thoughts into more calming ones.

Although it is best to seek guidance from a trained CBT coach, here's an exercise you can try for yourself.

First, you need to become aware of your stress-inducing thoughts. Pay attention to what's going through your mind when you're feeling stressed. Maybe it's thoughts like "I can't handle this" or "Everything is falling apart." Recognizing these thoughts is the first step.

Next, challenge those thoughts. Ask yourself, "Is this thought really true?" Most of the time, our stress-inducing thoughts are exaggerated or not entirely accurate. For instance, if you think, "I can't handle this," you can remind yourself of past situations where you managed just fine.

Now, replace those negative thoughts with more balanced and realistic ones. Instead of "I can't handle this," you could say, "This is challenging, but I have the skills to deal with it." This step is called cognitive restructuring because you're restructuring your thinking.

Practice is key. Keep identifying and challenging those stress-triggering thoughts regularly. Over time, it can become a habit to think in a more balanced and less stressful way.

BIOFEEDBACK AND STRESS

One intriguing approach to managing stress is through the use of biofeedback techniques. Biofeedback is a process that allows individuals to become more aware of their physiological functions and learn to control them. In this section, we will explore the concept of biofeedback and how it can be employed as a valuable tool to monitor and manage the physiological symptoms associated with stress.

Biofeedback techniques involve the use of various sensors and instruments to provide real-time information about bodily functions like heart rate, muscle tension, skin temperature, and even brainwave activity. By gaining insight into these physiological processes, individuals can learn to regulate them consciously.

Electromyography (EMG) is a common biofeedback method used to measure muscle tension. Imagine that your muscles are like rubber bands, and when you're stressed, these rubber bands tend to get tight and tense. EMG helps you see just how tight they've become. It does this by placing small sensors on your skin that pick up the electrical signals your muscles send out when they contract or tighten.

Research, like the study conducted by Chen et al. in 2019, has shown that using EMG in biofeedback training can be super helpful for reducing stress-related muscle tension and pain. This means that by using EMG biofeedback, people can learn to recognize when their muscles are getting too tense and then practice techniques to relax them.

When you're in a stressful situation, maybe a big presentation at work, and you start to feel your shoulders getting all tight and your neck getting stiff, with EMG biofeedback, you'd actually see on a screen how your muscle tension is increasing in real-time. This visual feedback can be like a wake-up call, helping you realize, "Hey, I need to relax my muscles."

Then, you can use relaxation techniques like deep breathing or progressive muscle relaxation to bring those rubber bands back to their normal, relaxed state. As you practice this over time, EMG biofeedback helps you get better at managing your muscle tension, which in turn can make you feel less stressed and more comfortable in tense situations.

EMG biofeedback is like having a little coach that shows you when your muscles are getting too tight due to stress and teaches you how to loosen them up, making you feel better in the process.

Another useful biofeedback tool is heart rate variability (HRV) biofeedback. Picture your heart as a metronome, ticking at a constant rate. However, when you're stressed, your heart doesn't always tick at a perfect rhythm; there are slight variations in the time between each beat. These variations are what HRV biofeedback pays attention to.

HRV biofeedback focuses on the changes in the time intervals between your heartbeats, and these changes can tell a lot about how your body is handling stress. The idea is that when your heart rate is more flexible, it reflects a body that can adapt better to stress.

When you practice HRV biofeedback, you learn to make those heart rate variations more balanced and harmonious. This, in turn, can enhance the balance of your autonomic nervous system, which controls many of your body's automatic functions like heart rate and digestion.

Another fascinating biofeedback method is neurofeedback, which focuses on the activity of your brainwaves. Think of your brain as a powerful computer with different programs running at different speeds. When you're stressed, these programs might start running too fast or too slow, causing problems like anxiety or even conditions like post-traumatic stress disorder (PTSD).

Neurofeedback helps you learn how to control these brainwave patterns. It's like teaching your brain to adjust its settings, much like you'd tweak a computer program for optimal performance.

Studies, such as the one conducted by Kluetsch et al. in 2014, have shown that neurofeedback can be incredibly useful for managing stress, anxiety, and even severe conditions like PTSD. By training your brain to find the right balance in its activity, you become more resilient to stressors.

Imagine you're someone who often gets overwhelmed by stress. With neurofeedback, you'd work with a therapist who uses sensors to monitor your brainwaves. When your brainwaves start going in a direction that indicates stress or anxiety, you'll receive real-time feedback – maybe a sound or a visual cue – that lets you know what's happening.

Over time, you'll learn techniques to shift your brainwave patterns back to a more relaxed and balanced state. It's like gaining control over your mental "dashboard," allowing you to respond to stress in a healthier way.

Biofeedback can be an incredibly valuable tool, especially for those who struggle to recognize the physical signs of stress within their own bodies. In essence, it acts as a bridge, helping you recognize and understand the physical symptoms of stress, even when you might not have been aware of them before. Whether it's reducing muscle tension with EMG biofeedback, enhancing autonomic nervous system balance with HRV biofeedback, or modulating brainwave patterns with neurofeedback, these methods empower you to take control of your stress responses.

ALTERNATIVE THERAPIES

While traditional approaches like exercise and meditation can help alleviate stress, some people explore alternative therapies to find relief. These therapies often focus on holistic well-being and have gained popularity in recent years. Although there are many different alternative therapies, here we will discuss some of the more popular ones for handling stress, including acupuncture, homeopathy and herbal supplements.

Acupuncture, an ancient Chinese practice, is gaining recognition as a stress management technique. The essence of acupuncture involves the gentle insertion of thin needles into specific points on the body, and it's grounded in the idea of balancing the body's energy flow, often referred to as chee. This concept suggests that when chee is in balance, the body functions harmoniously, reducing stress and promoting overall well-being.

Interestingly, research has uncovered evidence supporting acupuncture's potential to positively affect stress reduction. One notable study published in the Journal of Endocrinology in 2013 shed light on these effects. In this study, researchers examined the impact of acupuncture on stress hormones, particularly cortisol, which the body releases in response to stress. The findings were intriguing, as they suggested that acupuncture might help regulate cortisol levels. Additionally, the study indicated a reduction in anxiety levels among participants who underwent acupuncture sessions.

This research provides a glimpse into the potential benefits of acupuncture for managing stress. While the precise mechanisms behind acupuncture's stress-reducing effects are not yet fully understood, the evidence from studies like this one offers hope for those seeking alternative approaches to cope with the challenges of modern life. As with any therapeutic intervention, individual experiences with acupuncture may vary, and it's advisable to consult with a qualified acupuncture practitioner to determine if it may be a suitable option for your stress management needs.

Homeopathy, often regarded as an alternative therapy, takes a unique approach to address stress by using highly diluted substances to activate the body's innate healing mechanisms. This practice is based on the principle that "like cures like," meaning a substance that causes symptoms in a healthy person can, in highly diluted form, alleviate similar symptoms in someone who is unwell. In the context of stress, homeopathic remedies are designed to trigger the body's natural defenses and restore balance.

While some individuals have reported finding relief from stress through homeopathic treatments, it's important to note that scientific evidence supporting its effectiveness is somewhat limited. A systematic review conducted and published in the journal PLOS ONE in 2014 examined various studies on homeopathic treatments for anxiety and stress-related disorders. The results of this comprehensive review were inconclusive, indicating that there was no clear, consistent evidence to firmly establish the benefits of homeopathy in managing stress.

The inconclusive findings from this systematic review suggest that more research is needed to better understand the true benefits and mechanisms of homeopathic treatments for stress. It's essential to approach homeopathy with caution and to consider it as one of many potential options for stress management. As with any therapeutic approach, consulting with a healthcare professional who is knowledgeable about homeopathy can help you make informed decisions regarding its suitability for your specific needs and preferences.

Herbal supplements, known for their historical use in addressing various health issues, have also been explored as potential solutions for managing stress. Among these, adaptogenic herbs like Ashwagandha and Rhodiola rosea have gained attention for their perceived ability to reduce stress. These herbs are believed to help the body adapt to and cope with stressors more effectively.

A randomized controlled trial published in the journal Phytomedicine in 2017 investigated the effects of Ashwagandha supplementation on stress and anxiety levels in participants. The findings suggested that Ashwagandha had a positive impact, leading to reduced stress and anxiety.

However, it's crucial to approach herbal supplements with a degree of caution. These supplements, despite their potential benefits, can interact with medications and may not be suitable for everyone. It's highly advisable to seek guidance from a qualified healthcare professional before incorporating herbal supplements into your stress management regimen. Their expertise can help ensure that herbal supplements are safe and appropriate for your individual needs and circumstances, taking into account any potential interactions or contraindications.

Hypnotherapy harnesses the power of guided relaxation and focused attention to assist individuals in accessing their subconscious mind and making positive changes in their lives. Unlike the common portrayal of hypnosis in movies and entertainment, hypnotherapy is a therapeutic technique aimed at helping individuals overcome various challenges, including stress-related issues such as anxiety and phobias.

During a hypnotherapy session, a trained hypnotherapist induces a state of deep relaxation in the client. In this relaxed state, the individual becomes highly receptive to suggestions and is more open to exploring their subconscious mind. This is often referred to as a state of heightened suggestibility. The therapist may use verbal cues and imagery to guide the individual's thoughts and perceptions toward specific goals, such as reducing stress or managing anxiety.

Research into the effectiveness of hypnotherapy for stress-related issues has yielded promising results. Studies have shown that hypnotherapy can be a valuable tool in helping individuals manage and alleviate symptoms of stress, anxiety, and phobias.

The underlying principle of hypnotherapy is to tap into the subconscious mind, where deep-seated beliefs, emotions, and patterns are often stored. By addressing and reprogramming these subconscious elements, individuals can develop healthier coping mechanisms and responses to stressors. While hypnotherapy may not be the right fit for everyone, it has shown promise as an alternative therapy for those seeking relief from stress-related issues.

It's important to emphasize that hypnotherapy should only be conducted by trained and qualified hypnotherapists who adhere to ethical guidelines and standards. The therapeutic process is typically a collaborative one, with the client actively participating in setting goals and providing consent for the session.

Although there are many others, the last alternative therapy we will discuss is art therapy. Through engaging in creative activities such as painting, drawing, or sculpting, individuals can use art as a means to communicate and process their emotions, ultimately reducing stress and promoting overall well-being. Art therapy is often used as a complementary approach in stress management, working alongside other therapeutic techniques to address various emotional and psychological issues.

Research in the field of art therapy has shown that it can be effective in reducing stress and improving mental health. They have found that the act of creating art can trigger a relaxation response, reduce cortisol levels (a stress hormone), and promote feelings of calm and relaxation.

One of the strengths of art therapy is its versatility. It can be adapted to suit the individual's preferences and needs, making it an accessible therapeutic option for people of all ages and backgrounds. Whether it's through painting, drawing, collage, or other artistic mediums, the process of creating art can be a powerful tool for stress management and emotional healing.

Each type of stress therapy has its own potential benefits and evidence to support their use. Acupuncture may help regulate stress hormones, homeopathy's efficacy remains inconclusive and requires further research, herbal supplements like Ashwagandha show promise but should be used with caution, and so on. Remember, when considering these alternative therapies, it's essential to consult with a healthcare professional to determine the most suitable approach for your individual needs.

HORMESIS

Think of hormesis as the "what doesn't kill you makes you stronger" principle. It's a phenomenon where exposure to low levels of stress or toxins can actually have a beneficial effect on our bodies. So, a little bit of stress can be a good thing.

When you encounter stress, like exercise, your body responds by getting stronger. Studies have shown that regular, moderate exercise can improve your overall health, boost your immune system, and increase your endurance. This is an example of hormesis in action – a bit of stress leads to positive adaptations.

Now, let's talk about how this applies to other areas of life. Some researchers have found that consuming small amounts of certain substances, like caffeine or even alcohol, can have positive effects on health when used in moderation. For example, a moderate intake of caffeine has been linked to improved cognitive function and a reduced risk of certain diseases.

Hormesis isn't just about chemicals or substances. It also applies to mental stress. Facing challenges and overcoming them can build resilience and make you better equipped to handle future stressors. It's like a mental workout for your brain.

It's important to note that hormesis is all about finding the right balance. Too much stress, whether physical or mental, can have harmful effects on your health. It's about pushing your limits just enough to stimulate positive adaptations without overdoing it.

Hormesis is the concept that a little bit of stress can be good for you, whether it's from exercise, certain substances, or even facing challenges in life. Just remember to keep it in moderation and not go overboard with stress.

Now some ways you can incorporate hormesis into your life.

First of all, exercise. We have talked about this extensively already so we won't go into detail here, but all exercise is good for numerous reasons, including inducing hormesis. Another one we have already discussed at length is the use of meditation and mindfulness. We've also discussed nutrition, but in the world of hormesis, let's talk specifically about intermittent fasting.

Intermittent fasting is all about changing the timing of your meals to create short periods of fasting. This means you extend the time between your last meal of the day and your first meal the next day. For example, you might have dinner at 7 PM and then not eat again until 7 AM the following day. This approach introduces a mild form of calorie restriction, which can trigger hormesis.

Research has shown that intermittent fasting can have various positive effects on metabolic health. When you fast, your body experiences a brief period of stress because it's not getting a constant supply of food. This stress response can actually be beneficial. It stimulates the body to adapt by becoming more efficient in using its energy stores.

One of the key benefits of intermittent fasting is improved insulin sensitivity. This means your body becomes better at regulating blood sugar levels, which is essential for preventing conditions like type 2 diabetes. Studies have demonstrated that IF can help reduce insulin resistance, leading to better overall metabolic health.

Additionally, intermittent fasting has been linked to weight loss and fat loss. When you fast, your body taps into stored fat for energy, helping you shed excess pounds. This can also positively impact factors like blood pressure and cholesterol levels.

It's worth noting that intermittent fasting isn't suitable for everyone, and it's essential to consult with a healthcare professional before starting any fasting regimen, especially if you have underlying health conditions. People with certain medical conditions or who are pregnant or breastfeeding should approach intermittent fasting with caution.

Next, a couple of methods to induce hormesis using temperature. Cold exposure involves intentionally subjecting your body to cold temperatures, such as taking cold showers or baths.

One of the immediate benefits of cold exposure is improved circulation. When your body is exposed to cold, blood vessels constrict, and then when you warm up again, they dilate. This cycle of constriction and dilation can help enhance circulation, which is beneficial for overall cardiovascular health.

Cold exposure can also stimulate the production of norepinephrine, a hormone that plays a role in the body's "fight or flight" response. This hormonal response can increase alertness and energy levels, providing a natural boost to your day.

Furthermore, cold exposure has been associated with immune system enhancement. Some studies suggest that regularly exposing your body to cold stress can increase the production of white blood cells and other immune system components. This may contribute to a stronger immune system and better defense against illnesses.

It's important to note that while cold exposure can have positive effects, it's crucial to approach it gradually and safely. If you're new to cold exposure, start with mild temperatures and increase the coldness over time. Avoid prolonged exposure to extreme cold, as it can be harmful.

On the flipside, heat exposure can also induce hormesis. The most common way to do this is with sauna sessions. A big of regular sauna use is its positive impact on heart health. The heat stress from the sauna causes your heart rate to increase, simulating a mild cardiovascular workout. This can help improve circulation, lower blood pressure, and enhance overall heart function. Some studies have even shown that sauna sessions may reduce the risk of cardiovascular events.

Sauna sessions are also known for their relaxing properties. The heat promotes the release of endorphins, which are natural feel-good hormones, leading to reduced stress and improved mood. This relaxation aspect can be an excellent way to unwind and de-stress after a long day.

Moreover, saunas may assist in the detoxification process by promoting sweating. Sweating helps remove toxins and impurities from the body, which can be beneficial for overall health and well-being.

It's essential to remember that individual tolerance to heat varies. Therefore, start with shorter sessions, usually around 10 to 15 minutes, at lower temperatures, typically between 140°F to 160°F (60°C to 71°C). Over time, you can gradually increase both the duration and temperature to maximize the potential benefits.

Breath-holding exercises involve voluntarily holding your breath for a specific duration to increase your tolerance to reduced oxygen levels. This practice introduces a controlled form of stress to your body. To get started, it's essential to prioritize safety and begin with short holds, gradually working your way up to longer durations.

One of the primary benefits of breath-holding exercises is their potential to improve respiratory and lung function. When you hold your breath, your body adapts by becoming more efficient in utilizing available oxygen. This adaptation can lead to enhanced lung capacity and better oxygen utilization in your bloodstream.

Moreover, breath-holding exercises can train your body to remain calm in stressful situations, such as those that involve reduced oxygen availability. Learning to control your breath and remain composed under stress can be valuable in various real-life scenarios.

There's also evidence to suggest that breath-holding exercises may stimulate the production of red blood cells and improve oxygen-carrying capacity. This can contribute to improved endurance and overall physical performance.

However, it's crucial to emphasize safety when practicing breath-holding exercises. Starting with short holds, typically no longer than 15 to 30 seconds, is essential to avoid overexertion or oxygen deprivation. Gradually increase the duration over time and never push yourself to the point of discomfort or fainting.

Additionally, it's essential to practice breath-holding exercises in a safe environment, preferably sitting or lying down to prevent accidents in case you feel lightheaded.

STRESS MANAGEMENT TECHNIQUES FOR CHILDREN

Managing stress is important for people of all ages, including children. Just like adults, children can experience stress from various sources, such as school, family issues, and social pressures. However, it's essential to approach stress management for children differently than for adults. Children may not have the same coping skills or understanding of stress as adults, so we need to tailor stress management techniques to their needs. Here are some specific techniques that can help children manage stress effectively, based on research and expert recommendations.

Mindful coloring is a fantastic stress management technique for children. When kids color, they get to focus their attention on one thing - coloring inside the lines and making beautiful pictures. This focus helps their minds take a break from the things that might be stressing them out, like homework or problems with friends.

Scientific studies have looked into this, and they found that coloring activates parts of the brain that are responsible for creativity and calming down. This means when kids color, their brains start to relax and feel more peaceful. It's like a little vacation for their minds. Plus, coloring can be a lot of fun! Children can choose all sorts of colors and use their imagination to create wonderful artworks.

The best part is that when kids color, they might not even realize they're managing their stress. They're just having a good time with colors and paper. But at the same time, they're giving their minds a break from stress and anxiety. So, it's a simple yet super powerful tool that can help kids feel better when they're going through tough times.

Animal-assisted therapy is a special way to help children manage their stress. It's all about spending time with furry friends like therapy dogs or cats. When kids hang out with these animals, something magical happens in their bodies. Scientists have done studies and found that being around animals can make kids feel calmer. It's because when kids pet or play with therapy animals, their bodies produce oxytocin, the happiness hormone, which helps kids feel bonded and relaxed.

Animal-assisted therapy is becoming more popular in places like schools and therapy centers because it's so good at helping children cope with stress and anxiety. It's like having a special friend who can listen without judging, and who makes you feel safe and happy.

Breathing Buddies are another fantastic way to help children manage stress. It is basically teaching them how to do deep breathing. As you learned earlier, deep breathing is like a secret weapon against stress, and it can work wonders for kids too.

A Breathing Buddy can be a soft and cuddly stuffed animal or toy. Kids can put it on their tummy and then start taking slow, deep breaths. As they breathe in and out, they can watch the Breathing Buddy rise and fall with each breath. It's like a little game, but it's super calming.

Storytelling can be a magical way to help children manage stress. Kids are like little storytellers with their amazing imaginations, and we can use that creativity to help them feel better when they're stressed.

When children create and tell stories or go on imaginary journeys, it's like going on a mini vacation for their minds. They get to escape from the things that are bothering them, even if it's just for a little while. And research shows that doing this can actually lower their stress hormone levels called cortisol.

Parents and caregivers can join in on the fun and help kids create their own stories or adventures. It's like building a world where they can feel safe and relaxed. It's a bit like daydreaming but with a purpose – to help kids feel better when they're going through tough times.

Finally, sensory play is a fun way for kids to manage stress, and it's all about using their senses - touch, sight, smell, and hearing. When kids do things like playing with squishy kinetic sand, making colorful finger paintings, or exploring things with different textures, it can make them feel a lot better.

Like storytelling, sensory play allows children to forget about their worries for a while. It's really distracting in a good way. They start to focus on the here and now, which can help them stop thinking about the things that are stressing them out.

Helping children manage stress requires a different approach than that used for adults. Using techniques like mindful coloring, animal-assisted therapy, Breathing Buddies, storytelling, and sensory play can provide children with effective tools to cope with stress and anxiety. And in reality, adults can use them too!

CREATING YOUR STRESS MANAGEMENT PLAN

Now you have a good understanding of stress and the techniques you can use to mitigate it. Let's end by creating your personalized stress management plan. This can be extremely beneficial as it will help you deal with the ups and downs of life in a healthier way.

As you have learned, stress is a natural part of life, but when it piles up, it can really mess with your physical and mental health.

Although everyone can benefit from a stress management plan, there are certain groups of people who might find it even more helpful. For starters, those with high-stress jobs, like healthcare workers or first responders, can really benefit. Studies have shown that stress can lead to burnout in these professions, so having a plan to manage it is crucial.

Then there are students, especially during exam periods. Students who use stress management techniques tend to perform better academically and have fewer mental health issues. Parents, too, can benefit greatly, as the demands of parenting can be seriously stressful.

People dealing with chronic health conditions, like diabetes or hypertension, can also benefit from a stress management plan. Stress can make these conditions worse, so it's essential to have strategies in place to keep stress levels in check.

Lastly, if you've ever struggled with anxiety or depression, a stress management plan can be a game-changer. Studies have shown that stress management techniques can reduce symptoms and improve overall well-being in people with these conditions.

Okay, let's get into it.

Of course, I understand you're looking for more specific directions on creating a personalized stress management action plan.

Let's break it down step by step:

Step 1: Identify Your Stressors

Take some time to identify what's causing you stress in your life. It could be work, family, health, or other factors. Write down these stressors to get a clear picture.

Step 2: Set Clear Goals

Once you've identified your stressors, set specific and realistic goals for each one. For example, if work is stressing you out, a goal could be "reduce work-related stress by managing my workload more efficiently."

Step 3: Choose Stress-Reducing Activities

Select stress-reducing activities or techniques that work for you. This can include as many of the things mentioned previously as you like. Pick activities that you can realistically incorporate into your routine.

Step 4: Create a Schedule

Schedule these stress-reducing activities into your daily or weekly calendar. Treat them like important appointments. Research shows that scheduling can help ensure you make time for stress management.

Step 5: Healthy Eating Habits

Plan a balanced diet that includes plenty of fruits, vegetables, whole grains, lean proteins, and healthy fats. Avoid excessive caffeine and sugary foods, as they can contribute to stress.

Step 6: Prioritize Sleep

Establish a regular sleep schedule and create a relaxing bedtime routine. Aim for 7 to 9 hours of quality sleep each night. Adequate sleep can significantly reduce stress levels.

Step 7: Get some exercise

Make time for at least 30 minutes a day of exercise. Put this into your schedule.

Step 7: Reach Out for Support

Don't hesitate to reach out to friends, family, or a therapist when you need to talk or get support. Social connections are a valuable part of stress management.

Step 8: Time Management

Practice good time management by creating to-do lists, setting priorities, and avoiding overloading your schedule. This can help you stay organized and reduce stress.

Step 9: Monitor Your Progress

Regularly review your stress management plan. Keep a journal to track your stress levels and the effectiveness of your chosen techniques. Adjust your plan as needed.

Step 10: Stay Patient and Persistent

Reducing stress takes time and effort. Be patient with yourself and stay persistent in following your plan. Studies have shown that consistent efforts pay off in the long run.

Remember, this is your personalized stress management action plan, so feel free to adapt it to your unique needs and preferences. The key is to take proactive steps to manage stress and improve your overall well-being.

CONCLUSION

Stress, a universal human experience, is intricately linked to both our biology and environment. Stress hormones, like cortisol, play a pivotal role in our body's response to stress, acting as messengers that influence our physical and mental states. Recognizing stress triggers, which vary widely among individuals, is crucial for effective stress management. These triggers are shaped by an interplay of genetics, personality, and cultural influences, underlining the fact that stress is not just a personal experience but also a collective one.

The impact of stress on physical health is well-documented. Chronic stress can lead to a plethora of health issues, including heart disease, diabetes, and weakened immune function. Similarly, its influence on mental health is profound, often exacerbating conditions like depression and anxiety. In today's digital age, technology, while a boon in many respects, has also emerged as a significant stressor, contributing to information overload and a blurring of work-life boundaries.

Unfortunately, in an attempt to cope, many turn to unhealthy mechanisms like substance abuse or overeating, which only perpetuate a cycle of stress. Instead, creating environments that promote relaxation and support can significantly mitigate stress. This involves not just personal spaces but also workplaces, where stress management programs can lead to healthier, more productive employees.

Physical activity and proper nutrition are cornerstones of stress management, helping to regulate mood and improve overall health. Similarly, time management skills can alleviate the pressure of overwhelming responsibilities. Mind-body techniques like breathing exercises, progressive muscle relaxation, mindfulness, and meditation have shown remarkable efficacy in reducing stress. Cognitive Behavioral Techniques and biofeedback offer more structured approaches to understanding and altering our responses to stressors.

Alternative therapies and the concept of hormesis – the idea that exposure to low levels of stressors can be beneficial – are also gaining traction. Importantly, children, who are not immune to stress, require tailored strategies that consider their developmental stage.

Managing stress is not a one-size-fits-all endeavor. It requires a multifaceted approach, encompassing a broad spectrum of techniques from physical activities to psychological therapies. The key lies in identifying personal stressors and understanding individual responses to stress. By adopting a combination of strategies suited to personal needs and lifestyle, one can effectively manage stress, leading to improved health and well-being. In this journey, the role of a supportive environment, whether at home or work, cannot be overstated. As we move forward, it's imperative to acknowledge stress as a significant aspect of modern life and to equip ourselves with the tools necessary to navigate it effectively.

THANKS FOR READING

Dear reader,

Thank you for reading *Stress Management Tools: Coping with stress for mental and physical health and longevity.*

If you enjoyed this book, please leave a review where you bought it. It helps more than most people think.

Get the The Stress Buster Bundle For FREE!

www.FunctionalHealth.Coach/Stress-Buster-Bundle

Includes:

- Daily Stress relief Guide
- Stretch and Meditate Video Collection
- Stress Meter Interactive Quiz

Get them all FREE here: www.FunctionalHealth.Coach/Stress-Buster-Bundle

ABOUT SAM FURY

Health Coach - Content Creator - Optimist

www.SamFury.com

- amazon.com/author/samfury
- goodreads.com/SamFury
- facebook.com/SamFuryOfficial
- instagram.com/samfuryofficial
- youtube.com/@FunctionalHealthShow

REFERENCES

https://psycnet.apa.org/record/2002-02382-001

https://psycnet.apa.org/record/1986-01119-001

https://psycnet.apa.org/record/2003-03824-002

https://psycnet.apa.org/record/2014-22209-008

https://pubmed.ncbi.nlm.nih.gov/24341286/

https://pubmed.ncbi.nlm.nih.gov/27695158/

https://pubmed.ncbi.nlm.nih.gov/23124442/

https://contextualscience.org/publications/

https://www.ncbi.nlm.nih.gov/pmc/articles/PMC5004743/

https://www.scirp.org/reference/ReferencesPapers

https://pubmed.ncbi.nlm.nih.gov/14768970/

https://pubmed.ncbi.nlm.nih.gov/7751482/

https://pubmed.ncbi.nlm.nih.gov/23386059/

https://pubmed.ncbi.nlm.nih.gov/23439798/

https://pubmed.ncbi.nlm.nih.gov/24395196/

https://pubmed.ncbi.nlm.nih.gov/24266644/

https://pubmed.ncbi.nlm.nih.gov/25101026/

https://pubmed.ncbi.nlm.nih.gov/28279545/

https://pubmed.ncbi.nlm.nih.gov/31197192/

https://pubmed.ncbi.nlm.nih.gov/28279545/

https://pubmed.ncbi.nlm.nih.gov/25365629/

https://psycnet.apa.org/record/2016-45315-008

https://pubmed.ncbi.nlm.nih.gov/26170005/

https://pubmed.ncbi.nlm.nih.gov/28279545/

https://psycnet.apa.org/record/2017-07815-004

https://psycnet.apa.org/record/2017-07815-004

https://pubmed.ncbi.nlm.nih.gov/28279545/

https://psycnet.apa.org/record/2014-09380-003

https://pubmed.ncbi.nlm.nih.gov/24168779/

https://pubmed.ncbi.nlm.nih.gov/10195112/

https://pubmed.ncbi.nlm.nih.gov/7620309/

https://pubmed.ncbi.nlm.nih.gov/25771249/

https://pubmed.ncbi.nlm.nih.gov/18991954/

https://pubmed.ncbi.nlm.nih.gov/18154498/

https://pubmed.ncbi.nlm.nih.gov/12651993/

https://pubmed.ncbi.nlm.nih.gov/19481481/

https://pubmed.ncbi.nlm.nih.gov/23117636/

https://pubmed.ncbi.nlm.nih.gov/24168779/

https://pubmed.ncbi.nlm.nih.gov/23783199/

https://pubmed.ncbi.nlm.nih.gov/28065209/

https://pubmed.ncbi.nlm.nih.gov/15364186/

https://pubmed.ncbi.nlm.nih.gov/15250815/

https://pubmed.ncbi.nlm.nih.gov/15250815/

https://pubmed.ncbi.nlm.nih.gov/15364186/

https://pubmed.ncbi.nlm.nih.gov/17716090/

https://pubmed.ncbi.nlm.nih.gov/17925521/

https://pubmed.ncbi.nlm.nih.gov/10909877/

https://pubmed.ncbi.nlm.nih.gov/24050186/

https://pubmed.ncbi.nlm.nih.gov/16274443/

https://pubmed.ncbi.nlm.nih.gov/21199959/

https://pubmed.ncbi.nlm.nih.gov/12627048/

https://pubmed.ncbi.nlm.nih.gov/21199959/

https://pubmed.ncbi.nlm.nih.gov/12627048/

https://pubmed.ncbi.nlm.nih.gov/16274443/

https://pubmed.ncbi.nlm.nih.gov/15347534/

https://pubmed.ncbi.nlm.nih.gov/26361000/

https://selfdeterminationtheory.org/wp-content/

https://pubmed.ncbi.nlm.nih.gov/11894851/

https://pubmed.ncbi.nlm.nih.gov/25150681/

https://pubmed.ncbi.nlm.nih.gov/20652462/

https://pubmed.ncbi.nlm.nih.gov/3901065/

https://pubmed.ncbi.nlm.nih.gov/20652462/

https://pubmed.ncbi.nlm.nih.gov/3901065/

https://pubmed.ncbi.nlm.nih.gov/20668659/

https://pubmed.ncbi.nlm.nih.gov/14675803/

https://pubmed.ncbi.nlm.nih.gov/15554821/

https://pubmed.ncbi.nlm.nih.gov/24030837/

https://pubmed.ncbi.nlm.nih.gov/3901065/

https://pubmed.ncbi.nlm.nih.gov/19432513/

https://pubmed.ncbi.nlm.nih.gov/16639173/

https://pubmed.ncbi.nlm.nih.gov/25208008/

https://pubmed.ncbi.nlm.nih.gov/3901065/

https://pubmed.ncbi.nlm.nih.gov/17925521/

https://pubmed.ncbi.nlm.nih.gov/20806419/

https://www.scirp.org/reference/referencespapers

https://pubmed.ncbi.nlm.nih.gov/17716101/

https://psycnet.apa.org/record/2008-03751-008

https://www.researchgate.net/publication/318494444

https://psycnet.apa.org/record/2009-02015-032

https://scirp.org/reference/referencespapers?referenceid=751486

https://psycnet.apa.org/record/2011-10851-004

https://pubmed.ncbi.nlm.nih.gov/11518143/

https://friend.ucsd.edu/reasonableexpectations/

https://psycnet.apa.org/record/2012-09134-000

https://psycnet.apa.org/record/2006-21929-013

https://psycnet.apa.org/record/2012-09134-000

https://psycnet.apa.org/record/2006-21929-013

https://friend.ucsd.edu/reasonableexpectations/downloads/

https://pubmed.ncbi.nlm.nih.gov/19706386/

https://psycnet.apa.org/record/2012-21054-002

https://psycnet.apa.org/record/1997-05978-004

https://www.researchgate.net/publication/272775221

https://www.researchgate.net/publication/318494444

https://psycnet.apa.org/record/2008-03751-008

https://pubmed.ncbi.nlm.nih.gov/16248688/

https://pubmed.ncbi.nlm.nih.gov/15250815/

https://pubmed.ncbi.nlm.nih.gov/15448977/

https://pubmed.ncbi.nlm.nih.gov/11584549/

https://pubmed.ncbi.nlm.nih.gov/22254111/

https://pubmed.ncbi.nlm.nih.gov/24728141/

https://pubmed.ncbi.nlm.nih.gov/22894890/

https://pubmed.ncbi.nlm.nih.gov/16930802/

https://pubmed.ncbi.nlm.nih.gov/19810704/

https://pubmed.ncbi.nlm.nih.gov/16545403/

https://pubmed.ncbi.nlm.nih.gov/12499331/

https://pubmed.ncbi.nlm.nih.gov/28654669/

https://pubmed.ncbi.nlm.nih.gov/28654669/

https://pubmed.ncbi.nlm.nih.gov/19805699/

https://pubmed.ncbi.nlm.nih.gov/28428346/

https://pubmed.ncbi.nlm.nih.gov/20048020/

https://pubmed.ncbi.nlm.nih.gov/22775977/

https://pubmed.ncbi.nlm.nih.gov/28819746/

https://pubmed.ncbi.nlm.nih.gov/22820158/

https://pubmed.ncbi.nlm.nih.gov/29697885/

https://pubmed.ncbi.nlm.nih.gov/11148895/

https://pubmed.ncbi.nlm.nih.gov/22820158/

https://pubmed.ncbi.nlm.nih.gov/28819746/

https://pubmed.ncbi.nlm.nih.gov/11148895/

https://pubmed.ncbi.nlm.nih.gov/23630504/

https://pubmed.ncbi.nlm.nih.gov/21639664/

https://psycnet.apa.org/record/2003-03824-002

https://pubmed.ncbi.nlm.nih.gov/18954193/

https://pubmed.ncbi.nlm.nih.gov/21840289/

https://pubmed.ncbi.nlm.nih.gov/19432513/

https://psycnet.apa.org/record/2003-03824-002

https://pubmed.ncbi.nlm.nih.gov/7042457/

https://pubmed.ncbi.nlm.nih.gov/350747/

https://pubmed.ncbi.nlm.nih.gov/25710798/

https://pubmed.ncbi.nlm.nih.gov/18954193/

https://pubmed.ncbi.nlm.nih.gov/24395196/

https://pubmed.ncbi.nlm.nih.gov/24767614/

https://www.scirp.org/reference/ReferencesPapers

https://pubmed.ncbi.nlm.nih.gov/15141399/

https://pubmed.ncbi.nlm.nih.gov/14508023/

https://pubmed.ncbi.nlm.nih.gov/14508023/

https://pubmed.ncbi.nlm.nih.gov/14508023/

https://pubmed.ncbi.nlm.nih.gov/15750381/

https://pubmed.ncbi.nlm.nih.gov/16624497/

https://pubmed.ncbi.nlm.nih.gov/16460668/

https://psycnet.apa.org/record/2014-00756-008

https://pubmed.ncbi.nlm.nih.gov/11796077/

https://pubmed.ncbi.nlm.nih.gov/20150866/

https://pubmed.ncbi.nlm.nih.gov/16095639/

https://pubmed.ncbi.nlm.nih.gov/28796634/

https://pubmed.ncbi.nlm.nih.gov/15513768/

https://pubmed.ncbi.nlm.nih.gov/25018659/

https://pubmed.ncbi.nlm.nih.gov/25818837/

https://pubmed.ncbi.nlm.nih.gov/25883578/

https://pubmed.ncbi.nlm.nih.gov/22427383/

https://greenplantsforgreenbuildings.org/

https://psycnet.apa.org/record/2009-14684-001

https://pubmed.ncbi.nlm.nih.gov/24932139/

https://pubmed.ncbi.nlm.nih.gov/21415172/

https://pubmed.ncbi.nlm.nih.gov/14757721/

https://pubmed.ncbi.nlm.nih.gov/19934011/

https://pubmed.ncbi.nlm.nih.gov/28915435/

https://pubmed.ncbi.nlm.nih.gov/32112714/

https://psycnet.apa.org/record/2013-41289-004

https://pubmed.ncbi.nlm.nih.gov/28279545/

https://pubmed.ncbi.nlm.nih.gov/31256313/

https://pubmed.ncbi.nlm.nih.gov/24854804/

https://pubmed.ncbi.nlm.nih.gov/29696418/

https://www.samhsa.gov/newsroom/press-announcements/202110260320

https://nida.nih.gov/research-topics/addiction-science/

https://psycnet.apa.org/record/1984-17824-001

https://www.apa.org/news/press/releases/stress/
https://pubmed.ncbi.nlm.nih.gov/20015584/
https://pubmed.ncbi.nlm.nih.gov/23459093/
https://pubmed.ncbi.nlm.nih.gov/21534704/
https://pubmed.ncbi.nlm.nih.gov/19041187/
https://www.wilmarschaufeli.nl/publications/Schaufeli/197.pdf
https://pubmed.ncbi.nlm.nih.gov/9489272/
https://pubmed.ncbi.nlm.nih.gov/18662717/
https://pubmed.ncbi.nlm.nih.gov/16095639/
https://pubmed.ncbi.nlm.nih.gov/19382124/
https://pubmed.ncbi.nlm.nih.gov/21415172/
https://pubmed.ncbi.nlm.nih.gov/25535358/
https://pubmed.ncbi.nlm.nih.gov/21480706/
https://pubmed.ncbi.nlm.nih.gov/14757721/
https://pubmed.ncbi.nlm.nih.gov/24932139/
https://pubmed.ncbi.nlm.nih.gov/24607069/
https://psycnet.apa.org/record/1989-06961-001
https://pubmed.ncbi.nlm.nih.gov/4029107/
https://psycnet.apa.org/record/2007-05228-002
https://pubmed.ncbi.nlm.nih.gov/28279545/
https://pubmed.ncbi.nlm.nih.gov/17638488/
https://pubmed.ncbi.nlm.nih.gov/9489272/
https://pubmed.ncbi.nlm.nih.gov/3897551/
https://pubmed.ncbi.nlm.nih.gov/6668417/

https://psycnet.apa.org/record/2000-00794-002

https://pubmed.ncbi.nlm.nih.gov/9805281/

https://www.researchgate.net/publication/

https://pubmed.ncbi.nlm.nih.gov/22330730/

https://pubmed.ncbi.nlm.nih.gov/6737206/

https://www.scirp.org/reference/ReferencesPapers?ReferenceID=1927117

https://pubmed.ncbi.nlm.nih.gov/6059863/

https://pubmed.ncbi.nlm.nih.gov/15250815/

https://pubmed.ncbi.nlm.nih.gov/11818582/

https://pubmed.ncbi.nlm.nih.gov/24807831/

https://pubmed.ncbi.nlm.nih.gov/14769087/

https://pubmed.ncbi.nlm.nih.gov/17615391/

https://pubmed.ncbi.nlm.nih.gov/19488073/

https://pubmed.ncbi.nlm.nih.gov/17925521/

https://pubmed.ncbi.nlm.nih.gov/14757721/

https://pubmed.ncbi.nlm.nih.gov/12819225/

https://pubmed.ncbi.nlm.nih.gov/25705824/

https://pubmed.ncbi.nlm.nih.gov/21951023/

https://pubmed.ncbi.nlm.nih.gov/28833689/

https://pubmed.ncbi.nlm.nih.gov/17993252/

https://pubmed.ncbi.nlm.nih.gov/3766176/

https://pubmed.ncbi.nlm.nih.gov/15741046/

https://pubmed.ncbi.nlm.nih.gov/24993615/

https://pubmed.ncbi.nlm.nih.gov/15834665/

https://pubmed.ncbi.nlm.nih.gov/2248758/

https://pubmed.ncbi.nlm.nih.gov/15834665/

https://pubmed.ncbi.nlm.nih.gov/18089957/

https://www.scirp.org/reference/ReferencesPapers

https://pubmed.ncbi.nlm.nih.gov/23459093/

https://pubmed.ncbi.nlm.nih.gov/9613027/

https://pubmed.ncbi.nlm.nih.gov/24679399/

https://www.apa.org/topics/stress/body

https://www.mayoclinic.org/healthy-lifestyle/stress-management/in-depth/stress/art-20046037

https://www.health.harvard.edu/staying-healthy/understanding-the-stress-response

https://www.nimh.nih.gov/health/publications/stress/index.shtml

https://www.psychologytoday.com/us/blog/emotion-sociality/201609/sensory-play-helping-children-manage-stress

https://www.health.harvard.edu/blog/mindfulness-meditation-may-ease-anxiety-mental-stress-201401086967

https://www.apa.org/topics/stress/body

https://www.mayoclinic.org/healthy-lifestyle/stress-management/in-depth/stress/art-20046037

https://www.health.harvard.edu/staying-healthy/understanding-the-stress-response

https://www.ncbi.nlm.nih.gov/pmc/articles/PMC2568979

https://www.apa.org/pubs/journals/apl/

https://www.apa.org/helpcenter/stress

https://www.apa.org/topics/stress-relationships

https://www.apa.org/topics/financial-stress-health

https://www.apa.org/pubs/journals/ocp

https://www.mindlabinternational.com/press-release/weightless-by-marconi-union-named-most-relaxing-track-in-the-world/

www.ingramcontent.com/pod-product-compliance
Lightning Source LLC
Chambersburg PA
CBHW052154110526
44591CB00012B/1960